WITHDRAWN

Life Aboard a Space Station

Life Aboard a Space Station

Titles in The Way People Live series include:

Cowboys in the Old West
Games of Ancient Rome
Life Aboard the Space Shuttle
Life Among the Aztec
Life Among the Great Plains Indians
Life Among the Ibo Women of Nigeria
Life Among the Inca
Life Among the Indian Fighters
Life Among the Pirates
Life Among the Puritans
Life Among the Samurai
Life Among the Vikings
Life During the American Revolution
Life During the Black Death
Life During the Crusades
Life During the Dust Bowl
Life During the French Revolution
Life During the Gold Rush
Life During the Great Depression
Life During the Middle Ages
Life During the Renaissance
Life During the Roaring Twenties
Life During the Russian Revolution
Life During the Spanish Inquisition
Life in a California Mission
Life in a Japanese American Internment Camp
Life in a Medieval Castle
Life in a Medieval Monastery
Life in a Medieval Village
Life in America During the 1960s
Life in an Amish Community
Life in a Nazi Concentration Camp
Life in Ancient Athens
Life in Ancient China
Life in Ancient Egypt
Life in Ancient Greece
Life in Ancient Rome
Life in a Wild West Show
Life in Berlin
Life in Castro's Cuba
Life in Charles Dickens's England
Life in Communist Russia
Life in Genghis Khan's Mongolia
Life in Hong Kong
Life in Moscow
Life in the Amazon Rain Forest
Life in the American Colonies
Life in the Australian Outback
Life in the Elizabethan Theater
Life in the Hitler Youth
Life in the Negro Baseball League
Life in the North During the Civil War
Life in the South During the Civil War
Life in the Warsaw Ghetto
Life in Tokyo
Life in War-Torn Bosnia
Life of a Medieval Knight
Life of a Nazi Soldier
Life of a Roman Gladiator
Life of a Roman Slave
Life of a Roman Soldier
Life of a Slave on a Southern Plantation
Life on Alcatraz
Life on a Medieval Pilgrimage
Life on an African Slave Ship
Life on an Everest Expedition
Life on a New World Voyage
Life on an Indian Reservation
Life on Ellis Island
Life on the American Frontier
Life on the Oregon Trail
Life on the Pony Express
Life on the Underground Railroad
Life Under the Jim Crow Laws
Life Under the Taliban

Life Aboard a Space Station

by Michael Belfiore

LUCENT BOOKS
An imprint of Thomson Gale, a part of The Thomson Corporation

Detroit • New York • San Francisco • San Diego • New Haven, Conn. • Waterville, Maine • London • Munich

Hamilton Southeastern Jr. High

© 2005 Thomson Gale, a part of The Thomson Corporation.

Thomson and Star Logo are trademarks and Gale and Lucent Books are registered trademarks used herein under license.

For more information, contact
Lucent Books
27500 Drake Rd.
Farmington Hills, MI 48331-3535
Or you can visit our Internet site at http://www.gale.com

ALL RIGHTS RESERVED.
No part of this work covered by the copyright hereon may be reproduced or used in any form or by any means—graphic, electronic, or mechanical, including photocopying, recording, taping, Web distribution, or information storage retrieval systems—without the written permission of the publisher.

Every effort has been made to trace the owners of copyrighted material.

LIBRARY OF CONGRESS CATALOGING-IN-PUBLICATION DATA

Belfiore, Michael, 1969–
Life aboard a space station / by Michael Belfiore.
p. cm. -- (The way people live)
Includes bibliographical references and index.
ISBN 1-59018-460-2 (hard cover : alk. paper)
1. Manned space flight—Juvenile literature. 2. Space stations—Juvenile literature.
I. Title. II. Series.
TL873.B47 2004
629.45—dc22

2004010856

Printed in the United States of America

Contents

FOREWORD
Discovering the Humanity in Us All 8

INTRODUCTION
Mobile Homes in the Sky 10

CHAPTER ONE
Leaving the Planet 12

CHAPTER TWO
Arriving 24

CHAPTER THREE
Living in Space 35

CHAPTER FOUR
Working in Space 51

CHAPTER FIVE
Handling Emergencies 64

CHAPTER SIX
Surviving the Long Haul 75

CHAPTER SEVEN
Returning to Earth 85

Notes 97
For Further Reading 99
Works Consulted 101
Index 103
Picture Credits 111
About the Author 112

Foreword

Discovering the Humanity in Us All

Books in The Way People Live series focus on groups of people in a wide variety of circumstances, settings, and time periods. Some books focus on different cultural groups, others on people in a particular historical time period, while others cover people involved in a specific event. Each book emphasizes the daily routines, personal and historical struggles, and achievements of people from all walks of life.

To really understand any culture, it is necessary to strip the mind of the common notions we hold about groups of people. These stereotypes are the archenemies of learning. It does not even matter whether the stereotypes are positive or negative; they are confining and tight. Removing them is a challenge that is not easily met, as anyone who has ever tried it will admit. Ideas that do not fit into the templates we create are unwelcome visitors—ones we would prefer remain quietly in a corner or forgotten room.

The cowboy of the Old West is a good example of such confining roles. The cowboy was courageous, yet soft-spoken. His time (it is always a he, in our template) was spent alternatively saving a rancher's daughter from certain death on a runaway stagecoach, or shooting it out with rustlers. At times, of course, he was likely to get a little crazy in town after a trail drive, but for the most part, he was the epitome of inner strength. It is disconcerting to find out that the cowboy is human, even a bit childish. Can it really be true that cowboys would line up to help the cook on the trail drive grind coffee, just hoping he would give them a little stick of peppermint candy that came with the coffee shipment? The idea of tough cowboys vying with one another to help "Coosie" (as they called their cooks) for a bit of candy seems silly and out of place.

So is the vision of Eskimos playing video games and watching MTV, living in prefab housing in the Arctic. It just does not fit with what "Eskimo" means. We are far more comfortable with snow igloos and whale blubber, harpoons and kayaks.

Although the cultures dealt with in Lucent's The Way People Live series are often historically and socially well known, the emphasis is on the personal aspects of life. Groups of people, while unquestionably affected by their politics and their governmental structures, are more than those institutions. How do people in a particular time and place educate their children? What do they eat? And how do they build their houses? What kinds of work do they do? What kinds of games do they enjoy? The answers to these questions bring these cultures to life. People's lives are revealed in the particulars and only by knowing the particulars can we understand these cultures' will to survive and their moments of weakness and greatness.

This is not to say that understanding politics does not help to understand a culture. There is no question that the Warsaw ghetto, for example, was a culture that was brought about by the politics and social ideas of Adolf

Hitler and the Third Reich. But the Jews who were crowded together in the ghetto cannot be understood by the Reich's politics. Their life was a day-to-day battle for existence, and the creativity and methods they used to prolong their lives is a vital story of human perseverance that would be denied by focusing only on the institutions of Hitler's Germany. Knowing that children as young as five or six outwitted Nazi guards on a daily basis, that Jewish policemen helped the Germans control the ghetto, that children attended secret schools in the ghetto and even earned diplomas—these are the things that reveal the fabric of life, that can inspire, intrigue, and amaze.

Books in The Way People Live series allow both the casual reader and the student to see humans as victims, heroes, and onlookers. And although humans act in ways that can fill us with feelings of sorrow and revulsion, it is important to remember that "hero," "predator," and "victim" are dangerous terms. Heaping undue pity or praise on people reduces them to objects, and strips them of their humanity.

Seeing the Jews of Warsaw only as victims is to deny their humanity. Seeing them only as they appear in surviving photos, staring at the camera with infinite sadness, is limiting, both to them and to those who want to understand them. To an object of pity, the only appropriate response becomes "Those poor creatures!" and that reduces both the quality of their struggle and the depth of their despair. No one is served by such two-dimensional views of people and their cultures.

With this in mind, The Way People Live series strives to flesh out the traditional, two-dimensional views of people in various cultures and historical circumstances. Using a wide variety of primary quotations—the words not only of the politicians and government leaders, but of the real people whose lives are being examined—each book in the series attempts to show an honest and complete picture of a culture removed from our own by time or space.

By examining cultures in this way, the reader will notice not only the glaring differences from his or her own culture, but also will be struck by the similarities. For indeed, people share common needs—warmth, good company, stability, and affirmation from others. Ultimately, seeing how people really live, or have lived, can only enrich our understanding of ourselves.

Introduction

Mobile Homes in the Sky

Space stations were initially envisioned by scientists and science fiction writers as great wheels in the sky inhabited by dozens of crew members studying Earth from afar, conducting scientific research, and eventually building interplanetary spacecraft that would take explorers to the moon, to Mars, and beyond. These orbital outposts would slowly spin like giant centrifuges to provide Earth-normal gravity to their inhabitants and set the stage for permanent colonies in space.

While this is certainly possible in the future, the space station we have today is much more modest by comparison. The International Space Station (ISS) is of the same basic design pioneered by the world's first space station, *Salyut-1,* which was launched by the Soviet Union in 1971. *Salyut-1* and all the other stations that have followed, including the current ISS, are modular in nature, more like mobile homes in the sky than the orbiting skyscrapers imagined in the 1950s. The cylindrical modules, each the size of a small room, are launched one at a time, using either a rocket or a space shuttle, and connected together by pairs of astronauts serving as cosmic construction workers. Although the ISS is the largest space station ever built, it can hold only half a dozen astronauts at a time, and its normal crew complement is half that.

But while the space stations that have been built may fall short of yesterday's dreams in some respects, they have fulfilled many of the prophecies of the scientists and writers whose visions made them possible. Space stations have indeed served as orbital laboratories, enabling us to learn how to adapt to space in preparation for long-duration space voyages during which we will travel to Mars and beyond. They have served as homes in space for astronauts for more than a year at a time, providing valuable insights into what will be required for astronauts making the months-long journey to Mars and back.

Space stations give us a view of the universe unclouded by Earth's distorting ocean of air, and the weightless environment of a non-spinning space station allows astronauts and scientists to conduct experiments under conditions impossible to reproduce on Earth. The research being conducted on the International Space Station may well lead to lifesaving advances in medicine, as well as ways to manufacture alloys and crystals of unsurpassed purity.

Space stations are among the most complex engineering challenges ever undertaken, employing the world's best engineers and scientists in solving the problem of how to keep people alive and productive in space for as long as possible. This is a challenge individual nations have found impossible to meet alone, and so space stations have enabled us to reap yet another invaluable reward: international cooperation. The United States and Russia, locked in a bitter cold war for decades, finally found common ground in space, first cooperating on joint missions to Earth orbit in the 1970s and on missions to the Russian space station *Mir* in the 1990s, and finally collaborating with many other nations to begin building the International Space Station in the 1990s and 2000s.

But more than that, space stations have given us a perspective on our own planet that

The International Space Station was launched into orbit in December 2000. It is the largest space station ever built.

is not possible to achieve any other way. Astronauts returning to Earth teach us that life on Earth is more precious and more fragile than we can imagine. They show us that, when viewed from space, the peoples of the world are far more alike than they are different, and they admonish us not to take any part of life on planet Earth for granted. After living aboard a space station for six months, astronauts value as never before the feeling of grass under bare feet, the sound of water lapping against the shore, and the embrace of a loved one.

CHAPTER

1 Leaving the Planet

Before astronauts can be sent to a space station, they must pass a screening process and undergo extensive training at the facilities of one of the space agencies that will send them there. Only two space agencies can send astronauts to a space station: the National Aeronautics and Space Administration (NASA) in the United States and the Russian Space Agency (RSA) in Russia. Travelers who ride U.S. spacecraft are called astronauts, while travelers who ride RSA spacecraft are called cosmonauts. For simplicity's sake, this book will generally refer to all space travelers as astronauts. Astronaut training covers how to operate spacecraft systems; all aspects of launch and return, including emergency landings; and how to use and maintain the various systems aboard the space station.

The Right Stuff

Astronaut candidates must meet certain physical and psychological requirements to ensure that they can tolerate the rigors of space travel. NASA astronauts must have uncorrected vision of 20/200 or better, correctable with glasses or contacts to 20/20. They must have blood pressure no higher than 140/90, measured when they are sitting. They must be between 58.5 and 76 inches in height, and they must have no chronic health problems.

There are no formal requirements for athletic fitness, although astronauts are expected to be generally physically fit and to stay in shape throughout their careers as astronauts. Workout equipment is made available to astronaut candidates during their training, and they are encouraged to use it.

Candidates must also pass psychological screening to ensure that they have no mental health issues, such as substance abuse problems, that might endanger themselves or their colleagues in space. They must also demonstrate not only that they are self-reliant and able to react quickly and independently in emergencies, but also that they can work well with other people.

Astronaut School

If the physical and psychological criteria are met, astronauts undergo a training program that normally lasts at least two years. In addition to training for their stays aboard a space station, astronauts must become experts in the operation of the spacecraft that will take them to and from the station. This aspect of their training is identical to that of astronauts whose missions do not include living aboard space stations.

NASA astronauts are trained at the Johnson Space Center (JSC) near Houston, Texas, while RSA cosmonauts are trained at Star City, Russia. The training includes many hours of lectures on spacecraft systems, rocket technology, and basic science and physics. The lecture component of training is not always popular among astronauts. Astronaut Jerry M. Linenger described classroom training for his ride in the shuttle:

> We were imprisoned in a classroom for eight or nine hours of nonstop lectures. A different engineer would enter our cell every two hours. In excruciatingly painful detail, and with uniformly monotone voices, the experts would explain how rockets work and what each of the two thousand switches in the shuttle do. . . . So much for the glamour of being an astronaut.[1]

In addition to his training at the JSC, Linenger also trained at Star City since he was to serve aboard a Russian space station. He found that Star City, with its overcrowded living quarters and lack of privacy and certain

An astronaut uses virtual reality to train for space flight. The astronauts' training program usually lasts for two years.

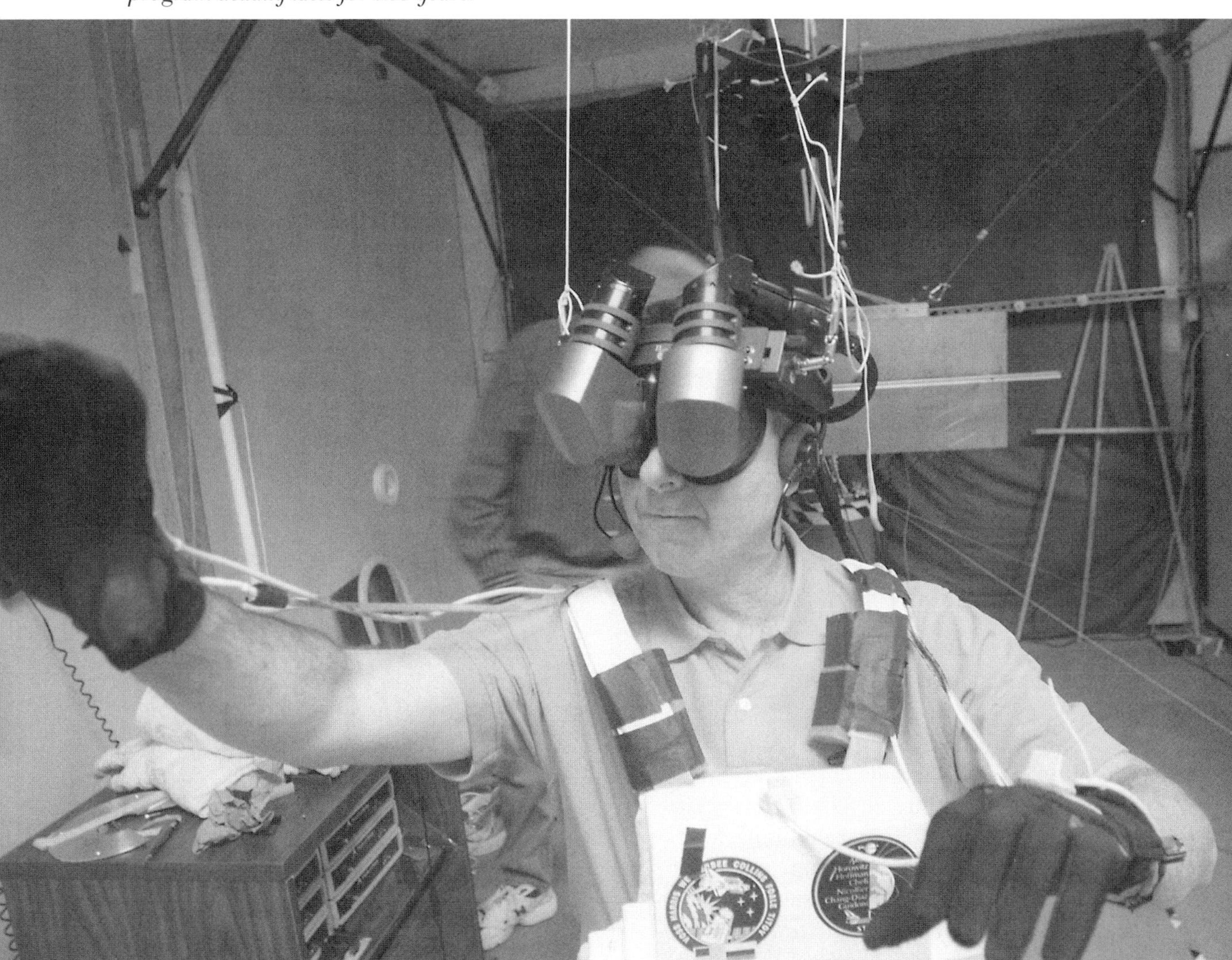

amenities, provided some informal additional training:

> Carved into the woods, thirty miles northeast of Moscow, the former top-secret military base was patrolled by KGB guards and only recently positioned on Russian maps. All phones were tapped; most still are. Star City residents live and work on the base. Nine-story apartment buildings are stuffed with people, four or five or six to a room. The heat for the entire compound is supplied from a central furnace, pumped out as steam to the outlying buildings. In order to save money, the furnace is not fired up until the temperature drops well below freezing, the rationale being that people can tolerate the cold for a few weeks. In the summer, hot water to all residents would be cut off for weeks in order to save on the Star City fuel bill. While uncomfortable, the conditions proved to be good training for space station *Mir,* where I would go nearly five months without a shower.[2]

Defying Gravity

At astronaut school, astronauts spend many hours practicing putting on and maneuvering in space suits. Since the suits weigh more than the astronauts themselves, the only way the astronauts can practice in them is to take advantage of the buoyancy of water. At the JSC, the candidates use a facility called the Sonny Carter Training Facility, or Neutral Buoyancy Laboratory (NBL). This 6.2-million-gallon, forty-foot-deep pool contains full-scale models of components of the space shuttle and space station to give astronauts the feeling of maneuvering during space walks. In the tank the astronauts are specially weighted to make them neutrally buoyant, which means they will neither sink to the bottom nor rise to the surface of the tank. Floating in the tank in their space suits, the astronauts can practice construction procedures, such as bolting station components together, and train for repair missions that will require them to open panels, remove broken equipment, and install new equipment.

The NBL can only simulate weightlessness, however. There is only one way that astronauts can truly experience weightlessness before they leave Earth: aboard a jet that produces conditions of weightlessness for periods of up to about thirty seconds by flying in parabolic arcs—first up at a 45-degree angle, and then over a gentle curve at high altitude for a downward plunge, also at a 45-degree angle. Flying several of these arcs an hour, astronauts can practice basic tasks that they will have to perform while in the weightless environment aboard a space station, such as eating and drinking. ABC News correspondent Kenneth Chang, while on a weightless training flight, experienced firsthand why the plane that produces weightless conditions is nicknamed the Vomit Comet:

> I lost it between the 33rd and 34th parabolas. Embarrassingly, it happened while the plane was flying straight and level, in normal . . . gravity. The up-and-down parabolas had paused for a couple of minutes as NASA officials fixed a glitch that had knocked out power to a couple of experiments.
>
> That's when my stomach decided breakfast had been down there long enough. I pulled out the little white bag out of the top-left corner of my flight suit.
>
> I threw up.

Two astronauts train underwater at the Neutral Buoyancy Laboratory (NBL) for work on the International Space Station. Training in the NBL simulates weightlessness.

> And that, thank you, was the only time I lost it. Hours after the plane touched ground again, though, I was still a little light-headed, a little queasy, pretty tired.[3]

Pulling Gs

In addition to learning how to cope with weightlessness, astronauts also train for the opposite—the crushing g forces they will experience when traveling to and from the space station.

The "g" in g forces stands for "gravity." Each g represents a force exerted on a human body equivalent to the pull of Earth's gravity. G forces multiply when a spacecraft rapidly accelerates to the speed necessary to achieve orbit and when it rapidly decelerates on the way back to Earth. These are the same forces auto passengers experience when accelerating onto a highway.

Passengers in an accelerating auto experience g forces only a fraction of the Earth's pull—enough to push them gently back into their seats. Astronauts on the way to Earth's

Orbit and Weightlessness

A space station can remain high above Earth without crashing to the ground because it is in a constant state of free fall. It is so high, and it falls so quickly, that it continually overshoots Earth's curved surface as it falls, in effect falling around the planet. Astronauts aboard space stations are falling around the curve of Earth along with the station, and this is why they, along with everything else in orbit, are weightless.

In order to achieve this state of equilibrium, or orbit, the space station must travel about five miles every second, or about 17,500 mph, and it must remain above Earth's atmosphere, above about one hundred miles. Below one hundred miles, atmospheric friction would slow the space station down below this crucial speed, and the station would crash to the ground.

Accelerating the components of a space station to 17,500 mph high above Earth's atmosphere requires a great deal of energy, but once the station is in orbit, little energy is required to keep it there. This is because, as Isaac Newton described in his first law of motion, an object in motion will stay in motion unless acted upon by an outside force (such as Earth's atmosphere).

orbit, however, experience sustained g forces equivalent to three to four times the pull of Earth's gravity. Under these conditions, blood pools in the body's lower extremities, depriving an unprepared astronaut's brain of oxygen and causing blackouts.

To train for experiencing the g forces of launch and reentry, astronauts training at Star City spend time in a centrifuge. This is essentially a giant merry-go-round that spins an astronaut rapidly, creating g forces. In the centrifuge, astronauts can practice "straining maneuvers" in which they strain their abdominal muscles to counteract the blood-pooling effects of high g forces. Some astronauts have a natural ability to cope well with high gs, as space journalist Keith Cowing pointed out about astronaut trainee Dennis Tito:

> One of the first symptoms one experiences on the path to blacking out during . . . centrifugation is progressive loss of peripheral vision. . . . At maximum acceleration Tito . . . didn't lose his peripheral vision. His trainers were rather startled and told him that he was the oldest person by far to have endured a ride on that centrifuge in such fine style.[4]

The Ultimate Video Game

At the heart of astronaut school is training in spacecraft and space station simulators and full-scale models, or mock-ups. In the simulators, the astronauts practice operating spacecraft and space station controls. Different simulators train astronauts to operate different sets of controls. Computers and human controllers determine how the simulators respond to the astronauts' commands. For instance, a space shuttle flight deck simulator takes astronauts through the procedures required for launch and landing of the shuttle. The simulator tilts up and down on hydraulic jacks, simulating as realistically as possible the motion astronauts experience during launch and landing. Computer-controlled views out the simulator's windows depict what the astronauts would see outside during different phases of flight, and the simulator even shakes and vibrates at the appropriate times. Human controllers test the astronauts by introducing emergencies, such as failure of different spacecraft systems, forcing the astronauts to respond quickly and decisively, just as they would during an actual mission.

Playing House

The mock-ups in which astronauts train are built to look very much like real spacecraft and space stations, both inside and out. Except for weightlessness, the mock-ups give astronauts in training the feeling of interacting with the real hardware during a spaceflight.

Four astronauts train at the Space Vehicle Mock-up facility in Houston. The mock-up is virtually identical to the spacecraft used in the mission.

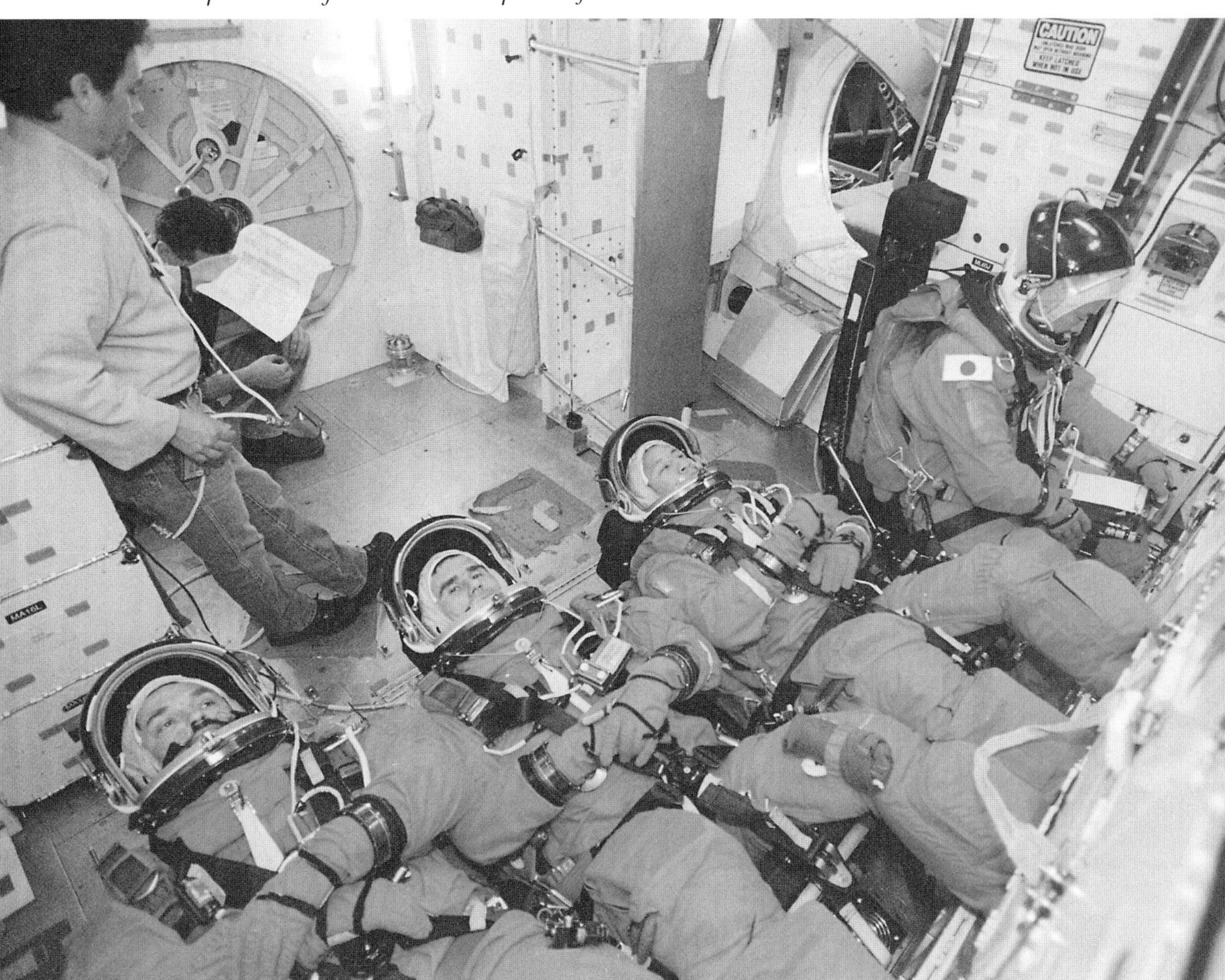

The mock-ups also allow astronauts to practice procedures for everyday living, which can be quite different in space. For example, astronauts practice preparing meals and entering and exiting a spacecraft while wearing space suits. They practice finding, using, and putting away scientific equipment, cameras, and other items, and they learn to perform basic housekeeping tasks. They even familiarize themselves with the operation of zero-gravity toilets—complicated mechanisms that use suction to contain waste that would otherwise float away.

Like the simulators, the mock-ups help the astronauts train for emergencies, such as loss of control during a spacecraft landing. The astronauts practice the procedures required for bailing out of a spacecraft while it is at high altitude in the atmosphere, and they also practice exiting a spacecraft that has been forced to make a water landing.

Since a spacecraft in trouble could come down almost anywhere in the world, including remote areas difficult for rescuers to reach, astronauts also undergo survival training in mountains, jungles, deserts, and the ocean.

The Big Day

Finally, after all the months of preparation, comes the day the astronauts have been waiting for: launch day. NASA's space shuttles launch from the Kennedy Space Center at

Space Vehicles

Two types of spacecraft are used to reach space stations. These are NASA's space shuttles and the Soyuz capsules of the Russian Space Agency (RSA).

The American space agency uses its fleet of three space shuttles to send crews to orbiting space stations. These rocket-powered space planes hold crews of up to seven astronauts and provide living quarters in low Earth orbit for up to two weeks at a time. These ships have been in use since the early 1980s. Space shuttles are mostly reusable and, in addition to the crew compartments, have an unpressurized cargo area for carrying large pieces of equipment such as space station components and satellites. They take off vertically, propelled by the thrust of their rocket engines and two strap-on booster rockets. Fuel for the rocket engines comes from a giant external fuel tank, which is discarded as the ship reaches space. The shuttle returns to Earth as an unpowered glider and lands on a runway.

Since the early 1970s, the RSA has used variations on the same basic spacecraft design for transporting crews to space stations. Carrying a crew of up to three astronauts, each Soyuz capsule is used once for liftoff and the return to Earth, and then discarded. Lacking the unpressurized cargo area of the shuttles, each Soyuz can carry only the crew and basic equipment and supplies. Although cramped by American standards, the Soyuz capsule, perched atop a several-story-high rocket at launch and returning on parachutes, has earned a reputation for extreme reliability unmatched by the U.S. shuttle fleet.

A third type of spacecraft, the Chinese Shenzhou, similar in design to the Soyuz, saw its first piloted flight in 2003. The craft is capable of reaching space stations and may in the future dock with the International Space Station or with future Chinese-built stations.

Cape Canaveral, Florida, while Russian Soyuz capsules launch from the Baikonur Cosmodrome in the country of Kazakhstan, next to Russia. Whether traveling aboard U.S. or Russian spacecraft, the experience is similar. Astronauts spend the night before launch, which can take place at any hour of the day or night, at sleeping quarters near the launchpad.

By tradition, the three astronauts who will travel aboard the Soyuz capsule observe a moment of silence before leaving their quarters at the Baikonur Cosmodrome. Before climbing aboard a bus that will take them to the launch area, the astronauts sign the door of their room, adding their signatures to those of dozens of other astronauts since 1975 who stayed in the room before them. Next, the Soyuz astronauts take a bus ride to the suiting-up area. Space suit technicians help the astronauts don their pressurized launch and reentry suits, and then, also according to tradition, the astronauts line up to salute the commander of the Cosmodrome and report that they are ready for launch. Although the spacecraft that takes the astronauts to the station is pressurized, both Soyuz and shuttle astronauts wear the suits to protect them in the event of an accidental depressurization of the ship as it thunders toward orbit.

One humorous tradition is still observed by male Soyuz astronauts as they take the final bus ride to the launchpad. When the bus is out of sight of the reporters and well-wishers, it stops, as it has done since 1961, when the world's first space traveler, Yuri Gagarin, took the first bus ride out to the launchpad. Like Gagarin before them, the space-suited astronauts climb out of the bus and walk to the rear of the vehicle, where they urinate on the right rear tire. Then they climb back aboard and complete the ride to the pad.

At the top of the rocket that will take them into space, the astronauts crawl on their hands and knees through the Soyuz hatch. From there, they lower themselves into the cockpit of the spacecraft, also known as the descent module. Astronaut Ed Lu described climbing into a Soyuz for his trip to the International Space Station, pointing out how cramped the ship is:

> In our bulky pressure suits it is difficult to maneuver into the seats and buckle up. . . . The Soyuz is a small, simple spacecraft—your basic no frills reliable ship. It was designed to do one thing, fly humans to and from an orbiting space station. That means it doesn't have to be large, just large enough to hold the cosmonauts and their equipment for however long it takes to rendezvous and dock with a space station. . . . We each have electronic displays so we can issue commands or look at status displays from the onboard sensors.[5]

When the astronauts have strapped into either their Soyuz or their shuttle, the technicians outside seal the hatch. Next the astronauts increase the air pressure in the ship so that it is just above the pressure of the atmosphere outside, and watch the pressure gauges carefully; any drop in pressure would signal a potentially dangerous leak in the ship. Once a proper seal has been confirmed, the astronauts test their radios and other communication equipment before settling back to wait for launch, which may be several hours away.

Blast Off!

The journey to a space station begins amid the thunder and fire of a rocket launch. Strapped into their seats aboard the spacecraft, travelers to a space station are shaken and deafened by the force of hundreds of thousands of pounds of thrust as they leave the launchpad.

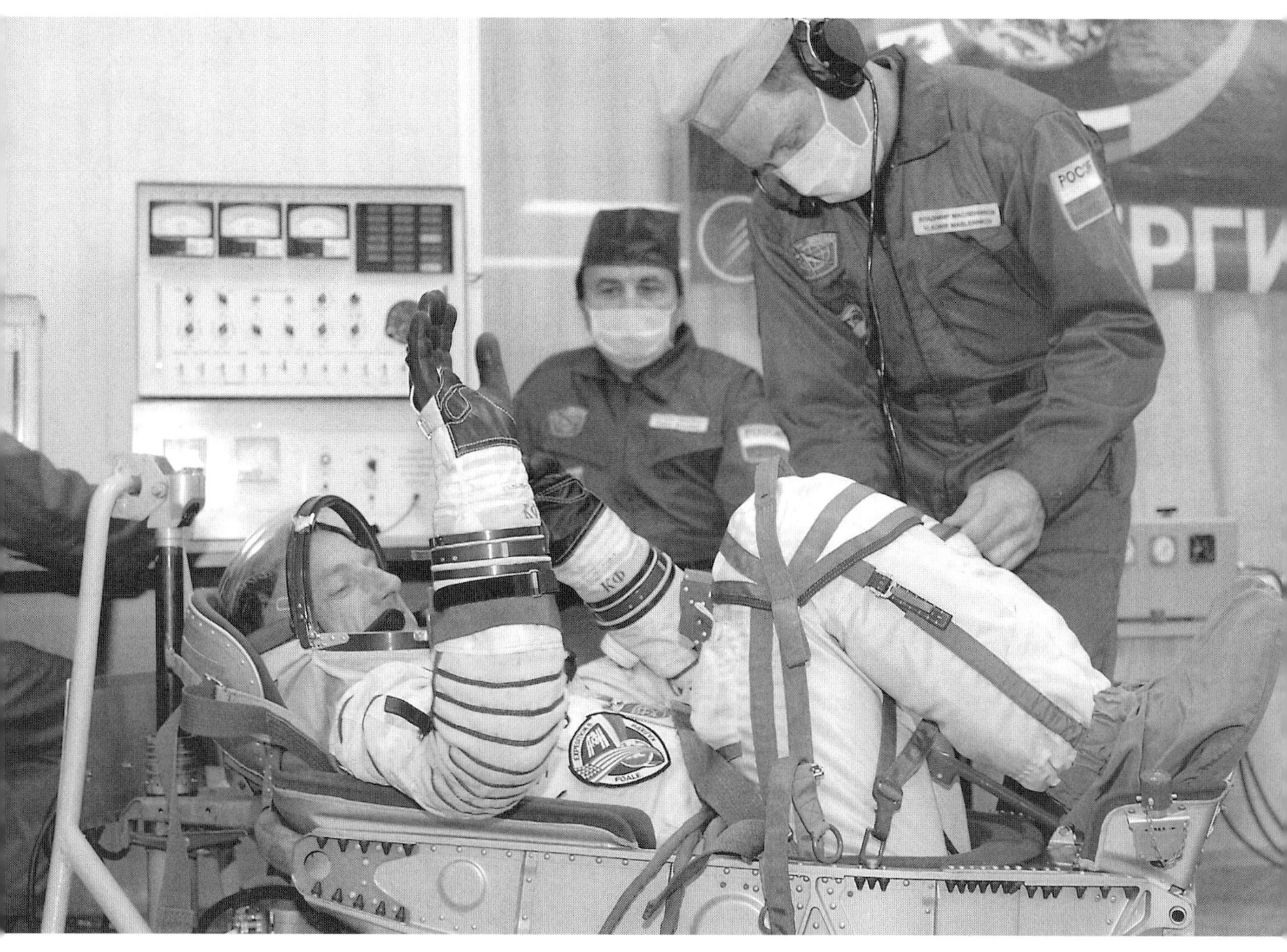

Technicians strap an astronaut into a Soyuz seat in preparation for blast off to the space station. The force of the launch can be overwhelming.

Linenger recalls his space shuttle launch to the space station *Mir:*

> I get slammed into my seat and, within seconds, I am flying upside down. The shuttle, after clearing the pad, rolls so it is inverted as it begins its journey up the East Coast. It is as if I were in the middle of a herd of charging buffalo. For the first two minutes of flight, with the massive boosters firing away, I also feel as if the shuttle would go wherever it wanted. Along merely for the ride, we were following the stampeded herd.[6]

Outside the spacecraft windows, the astronauts see the sky turn from light blue to deep blue, and finally to black as the craft leaves Earth's atmosphere and enters orbit. Soon after reaching orbit, the ship's engines shut off, and the astronauts become weightless. "Weightlessness," says Polish astronaut

Miroslav Hermaszewski, "comes on abruptly. I soared as if I were inside a soap bubble. Like an infant in the womb of my spacecraft, still a child of my Mother Earth."[7]

Small objects such as screws or other forgotten items may float out from behind instrument panels. If astronauts release their restraints, they will drift out of their seats and, with a small push, can travel through the air, as astronaut Joseph Allen did on board the space shuttle:

> When the engine shut down, I unbuckled myself from my seat and I was floating. I knew we were in orbit. We had to do an orbital-maneuvering-system (OMS) burn to get into a higher orbit. But before we even did the burn I floated upstairs—from middeck, below the flight deck—to look over [the other astronauts'] shoulders. I looked out the window and couldn't believe it. The sun was streaming in, and you could look right down at the Atlantic Ocean. I looked at . . . them doing the countdown for the OMS burn and I thought, How in the world can you do that? Look outside![8]

In Transit

Not long after reaching orbit, the astronauts can remove their bulky pressure suits and stow them, giving them more maneuvering room aboard the ship. This is especially important aboard the Soyuz, which is much smaller than the space shuttle. The Soyuz craft has only a little more than thirty cubic feet of habitable volume—barely enough space for three crew members. By contrast, the space shuttle can comfortably accommodate seven crew members.

During the two-day journey, the spacecraft performs a delicate orbital ballet to pursue, overtake, and finally dock with the space station. The

The Space Shuttle Disasters

The U.S. space shuttle fleet has suffered two cataclysmic accidents. In 1986 the space shuttle *Challenger* exploded as it headed toward space, destroying the vehicle and killing all seven crew members. In 2003 the shuttle *Columbia,* the oldest shuttle in the fleet, disintegrated while reentering Earth's atmosphere at the completion of a mission, again destroying the vehicle and killing all seven astronauts aboard.

In the wake of the 2003 *Columbia* disaster, NASA grounded its remaining fleet of three shuttles while it investigated the causes of the accident. The investigation was expected to take from several months to more than a year, and during that time NASA would not be able to send people into space. This left only the three-person Soyuz capsules of the RSA capable of reaching the International Space Station (ISS).

Meanwhile, questions were raised about whether NASA should try to fix the problems that had led to the latest accident, to develop a new space vehicle to replace the aging shuttles, or to undertake both projects at the same time. Some within the U.S. government, citing the reliability of the Russian Soyuz capsules, advocated a return to the simpler space capsule designs in use by NASA before the construction of the space shuttles. In any case, there remained little doubt that the U.S. government, with its investment of billions of dollars in the ISS, would eventually restore NASA's ability to send people into space.

transit time required to reach a space station gives the astronauts time to adapt to the weightless environment shared by the spacecraft and the space station. This period of adaptation is not always pleasant, as Russian astronaut Georgi Beregovoy explains:

> The first hours in space are no idyll [fun time]. You have the physical sensation of all your blood running to your head, which feels very heavy. When your eyes are closed it seems you are tumbling backwards. Either you are always floating up from somewhere or you are turning backward somersaults. There is an unusual lightness to your body, and your trained muscles seem to have no purpose. Your inner ear—the organ which gives you your sense of position—becomes

A Soyuz spacecraft prepares to dock with a space station. The astronauts become accustomed to weightlessness during the two-day trip to the station.

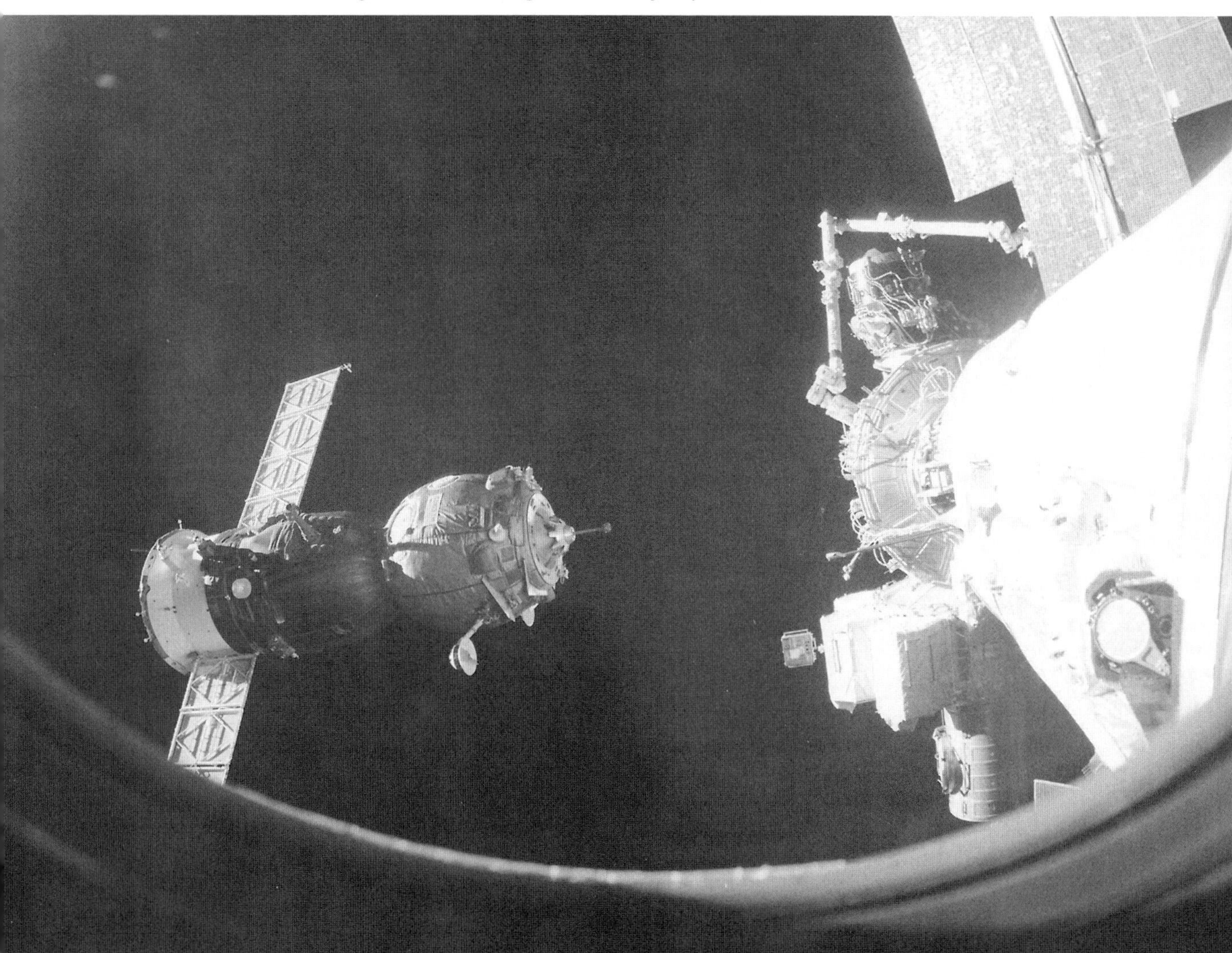

like a compass whose pointer has suddenly lost the Earth's poles. To begin with, you always want to hang on to something. You first hold on, letting go with trepidation, and then you find that there is nowhere to fall and that you simply hang in the same place.[9]

The Final Frontier

The transit time to reach the space station also gives travelers a chance to see Earth from space for the first time, and for many astronauts this is a profound experience. At a glance, an astronaut can take in thousands of miles of continent and ocean. Looking at the horizon, the astronaut can see the curve of the earth and the thin blue line of the atmosphere. Whirling around the planet at five miles per second, the astronauts witness sixteen sunrises and sunsets in a single day. "The sun," says Allen, "truly 'comes up like thunder,' and it sets just as fast. Each sunrise and sunset lasts only a few seconds. But in that time you see at least eight different bands of color come and go, from a brilliant red to the brightest and deepest blue."[10]

Astronauts have also described a heightened awareness of the fragility of the planet and the interconnectedness of all life on Earth. Political boundaries are not visible from space, and one's nationality becomes less important. Looking at Earth from space, says Russian astronaut Aleksandr Aleksandrov, "it struck me that we are all children of our Earth. It does not matter what country you look at. We are all Earth's children, and we should treat her as our Mother."[11]

CHAPTER

2 Arriving

On first reaching orbit, the spacecraft carrying crew members to the space station trails behind the station by about eleven thousand miles. Every hour and a half, the spacecraft makes one complete orbit around Earth, and because it is traveling faster than the station, each orbit brings it seven hundred miles closer to the space station. The spacecraft will not reach the space station until the third day of its mission.

Preparations

During the nearly sixteen orbits it takes their spacecraft to approach the space station, about 240 miles above Earth, the astronauts prepare their ship for docking. They also ready any cargo they are bringing to the station for transfer between the two craft. If the ship is a space shuttle, it may be transporting space station modules in its cargo bay. In this event the shuttle's payload specialist—the astronaut who is an expert in the handling and operation of the specific items the shuttle is carrying—must test the shuttle's robot arm, which is used to transfer large objects from the payload bay to the station. If their mission includes a space walk to install station components, the astronauts who will conduct the space walk use the time in transit to prepare the shuttle's airlock and their space suits for their excursion.

On the space shuttle, astronauts en route to a space station create drinking water as a by-product of the electricity generated by the shuttle's fuel cells. This process involves a controlled reaction between hydrogen and oxygen and creates more water than the shuttle's occupants need. The excess—some sixteen hundred pounds of it—is transferred to portable water bags. After docking, the bags will be carried by the astronauts into the space station. Although the bags are large and would be quite heavy on Earth, the weightless environment makes the transfer easy.

A Bright Star

About two days after the launch, the spacecraft draws near to the station. The astronauts aboard the spacecraft first see the space station when it is about forty miles away. Linenger described approaching the space station *Mir* in the space shuttle *Atlantis:* "As the solar panels of *Mir* reflected sunlight, the space station first appeared as a very bright star."[12]

Then, as the ship draws closer, the astronauts can begin to make out details of the orbiting outpost: "Eventually, the star became better defined, resembling a Tinker Toy–like monstrosity floating in space. As we moved in closer and closer, we began to see distinctly *Mir*'s six cylindrical modules."[13]

Matching orbits with the station at about twenty five times the speed of sound, the commander of the spacecraft lines up the ship for its final approach. The spacecraft may hover a short distance from the station to be sure that all is well before beginning the final approach.

Final Approach

The final approach is timed so that the station and the spacecraft will be in direct sunlight, rather than in Earth's shadow. This gives the commanders of the spacecraft and the station maximum visibility. The operation is also planned so that the orbiting outpost and the approaching spacecraft are in range of NASA or RSA tracking stations, ensuring that mission controllers on the ground can remain in constant communication with the astronauts during the docking procedure.

The space shuttle's cargo bay opens as it floats below a space station. Its payload will be transferred to the station via the shuttle's robotic arm.

Salyut-1

The world's first space station orbited Earth from April 19, 1971, to October 11, 1971. *Salyut-1* contained about thirty-two hundred cubic feet of living space, and, like all the space stations that came after it, was launched without a crew. The spacecraft of the first crew planned for the station failed to dock properly because of an equipment failure, and that crew was forced to return home without entering the station.

The station was finally occupied by Georgi Dobrovolsky, Viktor Patsayev, and Vladislav Volkov for a space duration record of twenty-three full days in June 1971. Their pioneering mission proved that human beings could survive and even thrive for long periods in weightless conditions.

The mission ended in tragedy, however, when the crew's Soyuz spacecraft suffered decompression after it undocked from the station for the return to Earth. Although the spacecraft's automatic systems executed a flawless return flight, the crew was exposed to the vacuum of space for twelve minutes. After the craft landed, the recovery team opened the Soyuz hatch to find the crew dead in their couches. Because of this accident, all spacecraft crews are now required to wear pressurized launch and reentry suits.

The first Soviet Salyut *space station was launched in April 1971.*

The approaching spacecraft fires its thrusters to move in, and the distance between the two craft narrows. The spacecraft's automatic rendezvous radar system continually monitors the distance to the station as well as the rate at which the two craft are approaching each other, or closing. To be absolutely certain that this information is correct, an astronaut on the spacecraft aims a handheld laser out a window at the space station. The beam of light hits the station and bounces back, allowing for an extremely reliable verification of the rendezvous radar system data.

The Soyuz spacecraft docks using an automatic system, but the pilot, or spacecraft commander, sitting in the middle of the ship's three seats, remains ready to take over manual control of the docking should anything go wrong. The space shuttles, on the other hand, always approach and dock under the manual control of the shuttle commander, who is chosen for his or her competence as a pilot.

The commander of the spacecraft must proceed carefully to ensure that exhaust from the ship's maneuvering thrusters does not hit the station's delicate solar panels, stretched out in a wingspan of 240 feet from the station's sides; any damage caused by the thrusters' high-velocity exhaust gases could reduce the panels' ability to gather sunlight. To further protect the station's solar panels, they may be maneuvered by the station's crew to a safe position out of the way and locked into place until the docking is completed.

"Go" for Docking

Thirty feet from the station, the spacecraft commander or the automatic system fires thrusters to bring the spacecraft to a hover relative to the station. This gives controllers on the ground a chance to make a final check of both the spacecraft and the station's systems to ensure that all systems are "go" for docking. Then, after receiving the go-ahead, the commander nudges the ship forward once more. Aided by a camera located on the ship's docking mechanism, the commander aims the ship slowly and carefully into the station's docking port. Inching slowly toward the station at a rate of less than a foot per second, the spacecraft commander bumps the docking port on the spacecraft against the docking port on the space station. This is called a soft dock.

Contact!

This final phase of the rendezvous is the most delicate, so it must be done extremely slowly. Even though objects in orbit are weightless, they still retain the mass they had on Earth. This means that even a slight nudge from a space shuttle, massing one hundred tons, could severely damage a space station, perhaps puncturing its hull and causing decompression. It could also damage the spacecraft itself. In fact, Soyuz crews put their pressure suits back on before attempting to dock, in case the ship's hull gets punctured during a docking gone wrong.

On the other hand, there is such a thing as being too careful; if the docking is executed too gently, the spacecraft and the station might not come together with enough force to latch them together. This is what happened when spacecraft commander Gerry Carr attempted his first docking with the *Skylab* space station in November 1973:

> When you get to around 50 feet, you reduce your closing rate to 1 foot per second or less. They really want you to make contact for the docking at slightly less than one foot per second. The first time we went in, we went in much too gently. We tapped it

Space shuttle and space station become one during the delicate docking procedure. To successfully dock, the two craft must be perfectly aligned.

so gently that the capture latches pushed us away and didn't latch. They were sprung, but they didn't capture onto the drogue [*Skylab*'s docking port], and they essentially pushed us away from the drogue. So we had to recock them and go back in and hit it a little harder the second time. . . . The second time I smacked it with a good one-foot-per-second closure rate, and it captured up just beautifully.[14]

Capture!

If all goes well, docking latches on the spacecraft and the station snap shut, drawing the two craft tightly together and creating a seal, called a hard dock. The spacecraft crew then report to ground controllers that they have achieved capture. Astronaut Norman Thagard described the sensations he experienced during the docking of a Soyuz spacecraft to *Mir:*

It was not violent. In fact, the way I describe it is if you've ever backed a car into a loading dock and they have those rubber cushions . . . it'd be about like that, kind of a little bump but nothing awesome, nothing scary. It's a definite contact, no question about it, as though you'd just bumped into something, but not a violent sort of collision.[15]

After their spaceship docks with the space station, the astronauts check the docking mechanism control panel to be sure that the two craft are indeed securely fastened together. Next, the crews of both the spacecraft and the station must verify that the seals between the two craft are airtight. Working from checklists, the spacecraft astronauts radio readouts of various pressure gauges to

Skylab

Built from hardware left over from NASA's Apollo moon missions, *Skylab* was America's first space station. It was launched on May 14, 1973, and remained in orbit until July 11, 1979. It had about 12,700 cubic feet of living space, or about four times the volume of *Salyut-1*. Its primary mission was to gather data about humans' ability to adapt to long-duration spaceflight and to conduct scientific observations of the sun and Earth, using sophisticated sensing instruments.

Skylab was occupied between May 1973 and February 1974 by three separate three-person crews, and it marked NASA's first foray into long-duration spaceflight. During *Skylab*'s last mission, astronauts Gerry Carr, Ed Gibson, and Bill Pogue set a space duration record of eighty-four days.

Skylab *was America's first space station. It was launched in May 1973.*

the station crew. Then the station crew does the same at their end.

A Hearty Welcome

Finally, after ground controllers are satisfied that there are no pressure leaks in the mechanisms connecting the ship and the station, the two crews get the "go" to open the hatches separating them and allow the atmospheres of the two craft to mingle. Linenger described the meeting of the *Atlantis* and *Mir* crews:

> Flying down the hatch I could see John Blaha, the American astronaut-cosmonaut whom I was about to replace, smiling broadly through the porthole. Although the hatch was still closed, the two crews could yell at each other and be understood.

A newly arrived cosmonaut opens the hatch of his Soyuz vehicle to enter the space station. Newcomers are often met with hugs and laughter.

> A friendly and talkative veteran of four previous space shuttle missions, John looked simply ecstatic to see us. As the hatch was swung open, John greeted us with a hearty "Welcome! Welcome to space station *Mir!*" followed by an uninhibited laugh. Then bedlam erupted, as the six of us blundered our way through the hatch and bumped heads with the much more graceful—being fully adapted to space—threesome of *Mir* occupants.
>
> The scene was one of hugs, shouts, mixed language [English and Russian], and laughter, feet dangling in all directions. Nine space-farers embracing and floating every which way. After the chaos calmed we all migrated single file—heads closely following feet—into *Mir.*[16]

Opening House

If the station is not occupied when a spacecraft arrives, it is up to the arriving astronauts to ready it for habitation, much like vacationers returning to a cottage in the spring. In a process that takes the entire first day aboard the station, the astronauts must establish a communications link between the station and ground controllers, charge the batteries on handheld equipment such as power tools, turn on food warmers, activate the toilets, power up the life support systems, and perform numerous other tasks to reactivate the station's basic systems from a powered-down state. Ground controllers, too, take part in the activation of the station. For instance, before the astronauts enter the station, the controllers send commands to the station to open valves on oxygen tanks, increasing the station's air pressure from a minimal level to the full pressure required by the crew.

Full activation of the station, including activation of the scientific equipment on board, can take several days. Recalled Carr of the list of procedures required to fully power up *Skylab,* "That checklist was about as thick as a phonebook. A New York phone book."[17]

After the hatch has been opened, whether or not the station is occupied when they arrive, the crew must also run cables and an air duct from the station into the spacecraft through the open hatch. This allows the spacecraft to draw power and maintain good air circulation from the station's resources rather than draining its own batteries and life support systems. As part of this process, the spacecraft is also readied for a quick return to Earth in case an emergency forces the crew to evacuate.

Adjustments

The arriving astronauts, accustomed to the relatively fresh air of their ship, may notice the smells of the space station, which may have been in orbit for several years. Some astronauts have commented that stations at which they have arrived had a musty smell, much like that of a damp basement. *Mir* astronaut Michael Foale said shortly after entering the station for the first time that the station "smells fairly musty—not an allergy threat, but a noticeable old smell, rather like old books in an attic."[18]

Getting used to new smells is not the only adjustment the astronauts have to make. Astronaut Joe Kerwin, speaking of his time on *Skylab,* described some of the sensations that new arrivals to a space station experience:

> All one has to do is rotate one's body to a [new] orientation and whammo! What one thinks is up *is* up! It turns out that you carry with you your own body-oriented world, independent of everything else. *Up*

is over your head, *down* is below your feet, *right* is this way and *left* is that way, and you take this world around with you wherever you go.[19]

In the larger area of the space station, where astronauts are able to move freely, the disorientation produced by the lack of a fixed up or down becomes much more pronounced and can sometimes cause dizziness, headaches, or vomiting. These symptoms of space sickness usually fade after a few days aboard the station.

The human body undergoes other changes in response to weightlessness. Without gravity to pull the body's fluids downward, fluid tends to accumulate in the upper body, particularly in the head. As a result, astronauts may experience stuffiness in their sinuses, as though they have a cold. Their faces may also appear puffy. These symptoms diminish over time, as their bodies adapt to weightlessness. One longer-term effect, however, is a lengthening of the spine; without gravity acting to compress the spine, an astronaut stretches an inch or two while in space. This effect is not permanent, though, and astronauts lose this growth after they return to Earth.

Down to Business

Astronauts have little time to adjust to their new surroundings before getting down to business. One of the first tasks after arriving at the station is often for members of both the ship and station crews to conduct a joint press conference with reporters on the ground. Such public relations activities are an important part of the job of being an astronaut. Since the continued survival of the space station depends on the approval of funding from the countries involved in the effort, projecting an image of women and men doing vital work in their nations' interest is crucial.

Also high on the list of priorities is a formal safety briefing given by the space station commander to the new arrivals, providing the newcomers with the details of how to evacuate the station in case of an emergency, along with other important information. The current inhabitants will also brief the new arrivals on all aspects of the station's systems and show them where important items are stowed. Such briefings are indispensable; like any complex piece of machinery, the station and its various systems will have developed quirks that astronauts cannot adequately prepare for as part of their ground-based training.

Such quirks often show up even when a space station is new, and members of the first crew must seek these glitches out for themselves. It is also up to them to unstow gear on board the station that has been secured for the station's launch and to set up and test scientific equipment that will be used during their mission. In some cases the station will have sustained minor damage—the result of the stresses that occur during launch—and it will be up to the first station crew to make repairs.

Whether or not the station is inhabited when they arrive, the new crew has to begin the time-consuming work of unloading supplies from the spacecraft, including fresh water, food, and scientific equipment. The spacecraft may also take on materials from the station to be returned to Earth, including completed scientific experiments, old clothing, broken equipment, and garbage.

Home Away from Home

At the end of their first day in their new home, the newcomers are shown to their sleeping quarters. The sleeping quarters are little more

Mir

Launched in February 1986 and deorbited in March 2001, *Mir* was the longest-lived space station ever built. In its final configuration, it contained about thirteen thousand cubic feet of living space. During its fifteen years in orbit, the Russian station enabled its crews to set duration records for stays in space.

The station also saw the first large-scale cooperation of the U.S. and Russian space programs, with American space shuttles servicing the station and American astronauts spending many weeks at a time on the station alongside their Russian crewmates.

Mir followed six previous inhabited Russian space stations, and it set the stage for the construction of the International Space Station by giving engineers, mission planners, and astronauts the experience they needed for large space construction projects.

Mir *orbits the Earth.* Mir *was the longest-lived space station to date.*

than tiny closets with sleeping bags attached to a wall, but the astronauts don't mind; each sleeping nook has a porthole that provides an out-of-this-world view.

Although astronauts are strictly limited in the amount of personal gear they can bring aboard the station, there is room for a few things, such as photographs of family members and a small music player and CDs. These items must be secured to the walls of an astronaut's sleeping nook so they do not float away.

The astronauts soon find that the space station feels like home. Foale described settling into his new quarters in a letter he wrote

The International Space Station

The International Space Station (ISS) has been designed and assembled in orbit by a consortium of nations as the largest and most complex orbital outpost ever built. The station's first section, the Russian-built Zarya, was launched from the Baikonur Cosmodrome on November 19, 1998. A space shuttle brought the next module, Unity, the following month, and astronauts then entered the ISS for the first time. By 2003 the ISS, still under construction, had grown to seven permanently attached modules with a habitable volume of fifteen thousand cubic feet.

to his family from the Russian space station *Mir:*

> After docking yesterday, I moved over to Spektr [a module of *Mir*] and set up my Russian sleeping bag, and am now wearing only Russian clothing. I have given all my US laundry to the shuttle and am eating all my meals with Sasha and Vasily [Foale's space station crewmates] in the Base Block [*Mir*'s control module]. But of course the shuttle crew join us for evening meals, when it gets very merry. . . . The *Mir* is much more homey, especially in the older modules, and not sterile-looking like the shuttle.[20]

Goodbyes

After a stay of several days, the spacecraft prepares to return to Earth. One or more of the new arrivals stays aboard the station, while an equal number of station crew members straps into the empty seats in the spacecraft for the return to Earth. The hatches are sealed, safety checks are made, and the latches holding the two craft together are released. Springs in the docking mechanism gently push the spacecraft away from the station. Once disengaged from the station, the spacecraft fires maneuvering thrusters to pull away from the station, again taking care not to hit the station's solar panels with the exhaust. The astronauts left behind on the space station watch as the spacecraft departs. Linenger described his feelings of isolation as he watched *Atlantis* leave *Mir:*

> I gazed out the window until *Atlantis* was hundreds of miles distant and barely visible. As the Earth below darkened, the shuttle stood out all the more distinctly because her altitude allowed her to continue to catch rays from the sun. My final glimpse of the retreating space shuttle was that of a brilliant star, low and near to the curve of the darkened Earth. Then *Atlantis,* too, blinked into darkness.
>
> I took a deep breath, felt a pang of loneliness, squinted one more time in a vain attempt to resurrect *Atlantis* and my astronaut friends, now far gone. I closed the cover to the window. My stay in *Mir* had begun. It was now just two Russian cosmonauts and myself, left to fend for ourselves, far removed from home and Earth.[21]

CHAPTER 3

Living in Space

After the ship bringing new crew members to a space station departs, those left on board settle down to the routine of life aboard an orbiting outpost. Even the simplest of tasks, easy to perform on Earth, requires special procedures, equipment, training, and patience to perform in the weightless environment of a space station. In essence, once they get to space the astronauts have to relearn how to eat, how to clean themselves, how to brush their teeth, and even how to go to the bathroom. Some of these procedures can be approximated on Earth, but most cannot be mastered until the astronauts actually get to space.

Camping Two Hundred Miles Up

In some ways, living aboard a space station is like camping in a wilderness where every necessity must be carried in to the campsite—although in this case, even air must be brought along. But unlike a camping trip, the stay aboard a space station lasts for months. Space station residents, by necessity, think of the station as their home away from home.

And what a home it is. More than two hundred miles from Earth, with a view of entire continents and oceans rolling by at about five miles per second, space station inhabitants witness a sunrise and a sunset about every ninety minutes. It's no wonder that space station residents have described living aboard the station as a life-changing experience. Gerry Carr, commander of the final *Skylab* mission, put it this way:

> It's a wonderful experience and it makes you feel far more humble, and it also makes you more of an environmentalist. You become very, very concerned about the Earth's environment when you've had a chance to see it from a distance.[22]

Like campers, some space station residents enjoy the break from the mundane details of their lives back on Earth. *Mir* astronaut Shannon Lucid described a conversation she had with a friend after returning to Earth:

> My friend put it real well. She said, "Hmmm, for six months you didn't have to do any laundry, did you?"
>
> I said, "Nope, never did."
>
> She said, "You never wrote a check, did you?"
>
> I said, "Nope, never did."
>
> She said, "You didn't pay any bills."
>
> I said, "Nope, never did."
>
> She said, "Must have been a nice vacation, huh?"[23]

Flying Lessons

In addition to the initial adaptation to the weightless environment aboard a space station,

A Day in the Life

In an interview with the author in 2003, astronaut Shannon Lucid described a typical day on the Russian space station *Mir:*

"We would get up every day at 8:00 Moscow time. I would quickly wipe my face with a wet rag and brush my teeth and brush my hair. We would go in and have breakfast together and then we'd do the plan of the day—whatever had come up the evening before.

Then we'd have lunch—we'd exercise either before or right after lunch—and then do whatever the ground had told us to do, and then we'd eat our evening meal. There was always lots of stuff that needed to be done around the station that wasn't really timelined, like picking up all the trash, and organizing things and moving bags of stuff around so that you could work efficiently.

Just after the last comm pass, the commander, Yuri Onufrienko, would go over the timeline—what the Russians called the Form 24—that had been uplinked, just to make sure that we understood what we were going to do the next day.

After the last comm pass, we would all separate. I would generally have about an hour to myself, which I would spend in Spektr [one of the station's modules], and that's where I would read a book, or whatever I wanted to do. I always went to bed at 12:00."

American astronaut Shannon Lucid relaxes in midair aboard Mir. *During her stay, Lucid enjoyed a scant one hour of daily privacy.*

the residents have to get their "space legs." This process involves more than simply becoming acclimated to weightlessness; the astronauts have to learn how to get around the station without bumping into objects or each other.

It is a gradual process, and the astronauts may not even realize how adept they have become until visitors come up from Earth, and the old hands can see how clumsy the newcomers are by comparison. Astronauts who have been aboard the station for a period of weeks get around by flying from place to place, pushing off from their starting location, aiming themselves just right so that they glide smoothly to their destination. Linenger explained:

> Up here, the three of us who are fully adapted to space fly from place to place by pushing off, very gingerly, and then doing a few midcourse corrections by either bending or twisting slightly. Sometimes, if I find myself deviating significantly from course, I might push ever so gently on a selected fixed object along the way. We brake again by finding a fixed object at the far end of the flight path and reacting against it.[24]

Newcomers, by contrast, often misjudge how much force is required, and at what angle, to push off from their starting point. As a consequence, they are more likely to collide with the other crew members, equipment, and the station's walls. In addition, as Linenger explained, "cords and cables along the flight path become handholds and are constantly being pulled out of their receptacles."[25]

Floating from place to place aboard the space station also makes it easy to unintentionally startle another crew member. With no floorboards to creak or footsteps to hear, astronauts often have no clue that another crew member is approaching from behind until he or she is upon them. The startled astronaut does not jump in the normal, Earthbound way, but he or she may gasp and flail his or her arms in surprise. At least one astronaut has admitted to deliberately sneaking up on his crewmates in this way, just because he enjoyed their startled reaction.

Astronaut Food

Since there is no gravity to hold things down, astronauts use care to prevent their food from getting away from them during meals. Mission planners help by selecting moist foods, since these tend to stick to eating implements rather than floating away. Foods that are less likely to crumble are also preferred. For example, astronauts keep crumbs to a minimum by eating tortillas instead of bread.

It is not possible to cook foods from scratch on a space station, so meals are prepared in kitchens on Earth and then sent to the station in pouches or cans. Some items are freeze-dried after they are prepared, and these meals must be reconstituted by the astronauts by adding hot water just before eating. Space stations have not in the past had refrigerators for food storage (though there are plans to add one to ISS), so food has been stored at room temperature. This means that fresh foods have been kept to a minimum.

The fresh fruit and vegetables brought up by supply ships offer a welcome change in the station crew's diet for a short time after their arrival. Lucid described what it was like to get fresh food after a long period of eating canned and processed food:

> I think I'd been up on *Mir* about three months when the first Progress [Russian

NASA Food Categories

TYPE	DEFINITION	EXAMPLES
Rehydratable	Food is dehydrated to reduce weight and preserve it longer. These foods require added water and soaking before they can be eaten.	Soups, casseroles such as macaroni and cheese, appetizers such as shrimp cocktail, and breakfast items like scrambled eggs
Thermostabilized	Bacteria and enzymes in food are destroyed by heat processing. The foods are packaged in single servings and can be easily cut open after preheating.	Grilled chicken and ham, tomatoes and eggplants, and puddings
Intermediate Moisture	By limiting the amount of water they are packaged with, these foods last longer without spoiling but still retain a soft texture. They can be eaten immediately.	Dried beef and dried fruit (peaches, pears, and apricots)
Natural Form	Ready to eat and packaged in pouches. They do not require processing.	Nuts, granola bars, and cookies
Irradiated Meat	Cooked meat packaged in pouches and sterilized with ionizing radiation. These foods remain edible even when stored at room temperatures.	Beef steak and smoked turkey

Source: NASA Life Sciences Data Archive (http://lsda.jsc.nasa.gov).

cargo ship] came, and we opened it up, and Yuri said, "Ah, you can just smell all the fresh fruit and vegetables that are here." So we dug around and we got those bags out, and for that lunch we had fresh tomatoes and onions. I think that was about one of the best meals I've ever eaten in my life. It was just great.[26]

For reasons that researchers do not fully understand, many astronauts find that their sense of taste is diminished in space. Because of this, much of the food that astronauts eat has been prepared to be very spicy—perhaps too spicy for their taste on Earth, but just right in space. Condiments such as ketchup, hot sauce, and salt and pepper are also available on board for the astronauts to spice up their food themselves. However, condiments that normally come in a dry form, including salt and pepper, are available only in liquid form on the station. This is to prevent them from floating away instead of sticking to the food. To use the liquid salt or pepper, the astronauts squeeze a drop of it from a dropper bottle onto their food, and then stir the food to mix it in thoroughly.

Which Way Is Up?

One unique feature of the condition of weightlessness is that there is no absolute up or down. What station residents perceive as being up or down depends solely on their position relative to their surroundings. This elastic perception of up and down can be disorientating for astronauts, even after weeks in space. For instance, some work spaces in a space station may be upside down relative to other sections, and moving from one to the other can cause momentary confusion. One might get up from the lunch table in the main part of the station and move into another module to exercise, only to find that the treadmill is attached to the ceiling!

Luckily, all it takes to reorient oneself is to simply flip around. Climbing on the treadmill, which suddenly appears to be on the floor rather than the ceiling, one again feels that everything is in its proper place—even though crewmates gathering around the table in the next module now appear to be upside down!

Astronaut Gerry Carr found this aspect of life in space one of the most difficult to get used to, as he explained in a 2003 interview with the author. Even after almost three months on *Skylab,* he still found himself "going from one module to another and having to catch myself and think a little bit, just for a few seconds, to reorient myself and make sure I was headed in the right direction."

This astronaut tries to orient himself aboard the ISS. "Up" and "down" become totally arbitrary in zero gravity.

Dinner Is Served

Food on the ISS is kept in a large, unrefrigerated locker. The cuisine is identified according to its nationality. Since the astronauts typically come from either of the two major nations participating in the project, Russia and the United States, the meals are stored in color-coded metal boxes—red for Russian meals and blue for American ones.

The astronauts can select whatever they want to eat from the food storage locker—chicken with rice and smoked turkey are two typical menu items—and then prepare them according to the way in which they are packaged. Some of the menu items require hydration—that is, the addition of water. These foods are prepared using a special faucet to squirt hot water into the container in which the food is packaged.

Meals that are not dehydrated come in either foil pouches or metal cans. Some foods are ready to eat right out of their packaging, while others, even though they can be eaten cold, are best if heated. To heat the food in the pouches, astronauts place them in a small electric oven. After about twenty minutes in the oven, the food is piping hot and ready to eat. This type of food is packaged and sterilized in foil pouches using the same technology used to produce food for soldiers in combat and even many foods found in supermarkets. As-

Two astronauts enjoy a meal in the zero-gravity space station. Each food item is foil-wrapped and labeled.

tronauts heat canned food, again before opening it, by placing it in a special heater built into the dining table.

To eat a meal after it has been heated, an astronaut cuts open one edge of the food pouch with a pair of scissors, or opens the can with an ordinary can opener, and eats the food directly out of the pouch or can with a spoon, keeping a napkin handy to catch any particles or juices that might drift away. Large particles that get away from the diner are chased down and eaten, much as a fish on Earth eats its dinner.

Hot and cold beverages, such as teas and fruit drinks, often come in powdered form in specially constructed pouches. A beverage pouch has a one-way valve on one end. An astronaut attaches the valve to either the hot- or cold-water nozzle in the dining area, depending on the type of drink, and then uses a control panel near the nozzle to select the amount of water needed to fill the pouch—typically 200 milliliters. Dispensing only the precise amount of water needed for a given purpose helps the station to conserve one of its most valuable resources. Finally, the astronaut shakes the pouch vigorously to thoroughly mix the drink powder with the water, and then snips off the end of the pouch opposite the valve to drink the beverage.

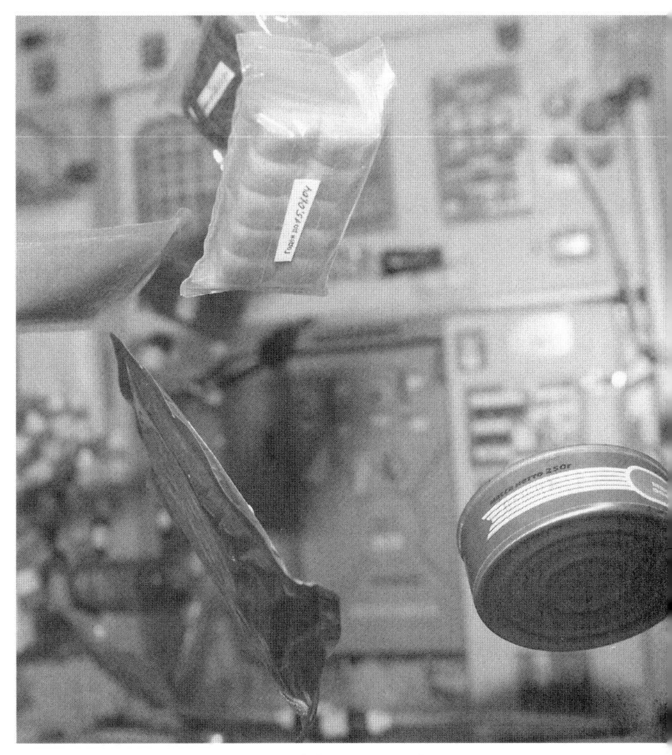

Cans and pouches of food hang in the air aboard the space station. Beverage pouches have one-way valves.

Space Toilet

Just as food preparation and consumption in orbit require special procedures, using the toilet is different than it is on Earth. In the absence of gravity, an astronaut must use restraints to stay attached to the toilet. When the astronaut is finished using the toilet, he or she then activates a vacuum-cleaner-like system to suck solid wastes into a holding container, where they can be disposed of on a shuttle or a Progress cargo ship. Urine is treated differently than solid waste. Water is a precious commodity aboard a space station, so astronauts must urinate into a hose that sucks the urine into a tank, where the water within it is recycled.

Mir astronaut Michael Foale responded in a letter to the concerns of his Earthbound colleagues, who were awaiting their turns to live on the space station and wanted to be sure they would be comfortable using the station's toilet:

> Yes, the toilet is pretty good. It is easier to do number twos than the Shuttle's, but it still takes me a good fifteen to twenty minutes from start to finish. I ration myself to once a day, because it is so time-costly.[27]

Rub a Dub

Because water is so precious (every gallon of it costs more than $83,000 to transport from Earth, so the space agencies send no more than is absolutely necessary), astronauts use as little as possible to keep clean. Once a day they use moistened washcloths to bathe, and they usually do not wash their clothes at all. They can, however, shampoo their hair using a special shampoo that does not require rinsing. The shampoo was originally developed for hospital patients who are unable to get out of bed to use a shower, but it works just as well for astronauts. Every ten days or so, the astronauts have a chance to take a shower in a special space shower. The shower is completely enclosed to prevent blobs of water from floating around the station, where they would not only be unpleasant to run into, but could harm electrical equipment.

After sealing the shower at the floor and the ceiling of the station, astronauts squirt themselves with water from a pressurized bottle, and then rub the water and some soap around on their bodies. Since the water will not drain away due to the lack of gravity, the soapy water must be sucked away with a vacuum cleaner and later placed in wastewater tanks. To finish, the astronauts rinse off with more water from the pressurized bottle, again vacuuming up the water when finished.

Shave and a Haircut

Like bathing, other personal grooming activities also require special procedures in a weightless environment. Hair and beards grow just as they do on Earth, and must be cut. The astronauts cut each other's hair every few weeks at least, and must take care that the hair clippings do not get loose and float around the station, where they could be inhaled or stick in someone's eye. To prevent loose hair clippings from flying around, the person cutting hair holds the scissors in one hand and a vacuum cleaner in the other, vacuuming up the clippings as they are cut.

Shaving presents a more difficult problem, and it is one that some space station residents have chosen to avoid all together. "Shaving wasn't really all that easy to do and it wasn't all that satisfying," explained Carr of his experience aboard *Skylab*. "[Crewmate] Bill [Pouge] and I just decided to go ahead a let our beards go. [Crewmate] Ed [Gibson] doesn't have a whole lot of facial hair, so it wasn't any problem at all for him either way." Carr described the shaving implements he and his crewmates had aboard the station and why they weren't up to the job:

> We had a little mechanical windup razor, and it didn't work as well as we liked. It was not good at all. We also had Mennon brushless shavers, as I remember, with razor blades in them. But the trouble with that brushless shaver stuff is that you can't just put your razor under a faucet and shake it and get all that stuff off of it. The only way to get it off was to wipe it off, and of course that dulled the blade.[28]

Taking Out the Laundry

There are no washing machines and clothes driers on a space station. It is possible to wash clothing by hand, using a large plastic bag in place of a sink, but this is a very time-consuming process, so astronauts rarely bother. Instead, clothes are usually worn until they smell, at which point they are placed with other trash for disposal on an empty supply ship.

Space station astronauts change their underwear—the same type they wear on Earth—

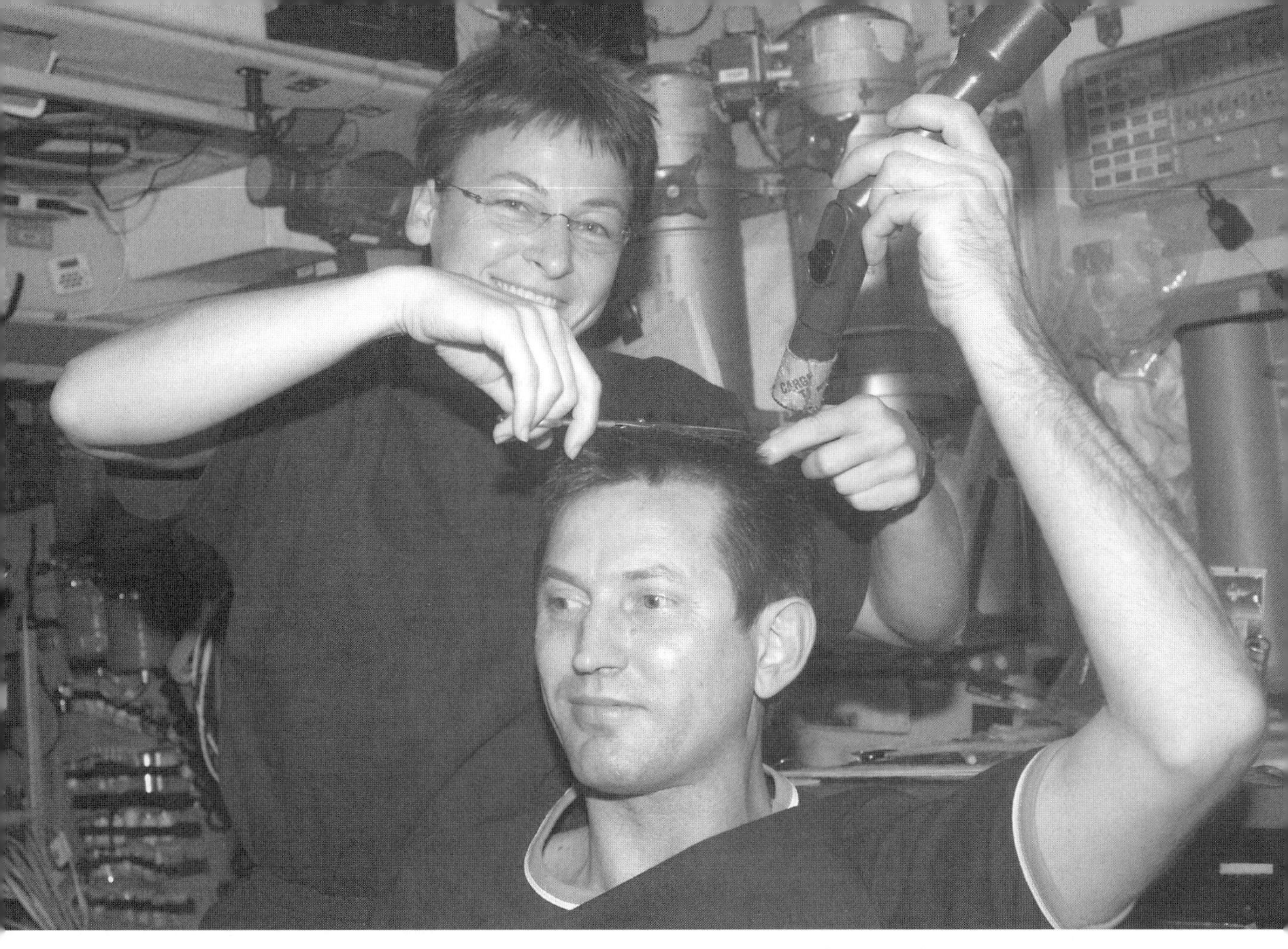

An astronaut vacuums his hair out of the air as his colleague cuts it off. Personal grooming in zero gravity calls for special procedures.

once a day, throwing away the old pairs. On average, space station residents change their outer garments every three days or so. They keep a special set of clothes as clean as possible to wear for on-camera news conferences and other special occasions. Before soiled clothing is discarded, it is hung up to dry along the station's walls. This allows the station's dehumidifiers to absorb and recycle the moisture from the clothing.

Discarded clothes, empty food containers, broken equipment, and other trash is first stored in a dedicated area of the space station, and then it is placed in an empty cargo ship that has remained docked to the station after delivering supplies. When the ship is full of garbage, the astronauts seal the hatch and jettison the ship. The ship flies on autopilot away from the station and then drops out of orbit and burns up as it reenters Earth's atmosphere. Linenger described the departure of a cargo ship from *Mir:*

> Today, I sat directly in front of the hatch from which the Progress departed. I could both feel and hear the springs pushing it

away. When I looked out of a tiny window adjacent to the hatch, I could see three of the vessel's running lights moving away. The spacecraft was stable and slow-moving. I then saw the spacecraft thrusters firing, which put on a pretty neat light show.[29]

A space shuttle can also act as a garbage truck. After it has delivered needed supplies and exchanged crew members, it can haul away garbage stowed aboard the station at the end of its mission, which usually lasts ten days or so. In addition to garbage, the shuttle may also return reusable scientific equipment, the results of medical experiments, and other nondisposable items to Earth.

Housekeeping

As with any habitation, space stations require their occupants to perform housekeeping chores to keep them clean and in good repair. Like every other aspect of life on a space station, however, these chores are of a special nature, and often take up a good deal of the crew's time. In addition to vacuuming and scrubbing, station inhabitants must clean air filters and perform other maintenance procedures on life support equipment.

Although many of the housekeeping chores performed by space station residents are similar to those required of residents of ordinary houses, a space station is a spacecraft as well as

ISS residents use high-tech hardware to perform daily household tasks like cleaning, as well as for their scientific work.

a dwelling, and this imposes many additional duties on its inhabitants. A space station has thrusters, a robotic arm used for manipulating equipment and new station modules outside, communications equipment, solar panels that can be individually controlled, and many other systems that must be monitored and adjusted as part of the ordinary operation of the station. These systems are operated from a central location. Laptop computers running specialized software serve as control panels for most of the systems, with individual controls appearing on the screens as icons that can be manipulated by pointing and clicking with cursors.

Another special maintenance chore is boosting the station to a higher orbit. This must be done periodically because the station travels in a low Earth orbit, where there are still some rarified traces of the atmosphere. These atmospheric traces impact the station and slow it down over time. As the station slows down, its orbit begins to decay. Left to itself, the station would eventually lose enough altitude to drop out of orbit, reentering the atmosphere and burning up in a spectacular fireball in the process.

The boosting that prevents this from happening is accomplished by firing a large thruster to increase the station's velocity and restore it to a higher orbit. The acceleration is nowhere near as extreme as that experienced by astronauts during a launch from Earth. Instead, during the two minutes or so that the thruster fires, the astronauts notice a very slight—but definite—tendency for unsecured objects, including themselves, to drift toward the rear of the station. In fact, the acceleration is so slight that the astronauts do not bother securing any but the most delicate of their gear.

Another unique feature of space housekeeping is making sure the oxygen-generating system, called Elektron on the International Space Station, stays filled with water. The system works by running electricity through the water to split it into its component gases, oxygen and hydrogen, in a process known as electrolysis. Water for the Elektron system comes from containers kept in a large storage area aboard the station; electricity for the process is generated by the solar panels.

Cleaning House

Special care must be taken to keep the intake vents of the air circulation system free of debris. Anything floating loose in the station—nuts and bolts, hair, even particles of dead skin—inevitably gets sucked against the filters in the intake vents. Such debris can block the airflow and overload the air-conditioning system. Astronauts vacuum the intake vents regularly to keep the air circulating properly.

One benefit of the tendency of the intake vents to suck up loose objects is that items that are lost can often be found by examining the intake vents. "When vacuuming," said Linenger, "I always carry a lost-and-found bag for all the goodies that I gather. During the week, I never declare anything truly lost until after Saturday morning, since missing pens, tools, diskettes, toothbrushes, you name it, can usually be found in the filters."[30]

No matter how effective, the air filters cannot remove all microorganisms, such as mold and bacteria, from the air. Unless special steps are taken, the walls, handrails, and other surfaces in the station will become home to colonies of mold and bacteria. These growths are not only unattractive, they can pose a danger to the space station; as the colonies of microbes grow, they can eat away at the very walls of the station. The paint used on the walls contains fungicide, which inhibits the growth of microbes but does not stop it completely. So every week, astronauts wipe and scrub the walls with special towels soaked in antiseptic cleaning fluid. They may also scrape the walls for laboratory samples in order to test whether microbes are gaining a foothold on the walls.

Perhaps less hazardous than microorganisms, but still a major nuisance, is plain, old-fashioned clutter. Items brought on board tend to stay on board, even after they have outlived their usefulness—unless room can be found for them aboard an empty cargo ship. Since there is little space for storage of outdated materials and equipment, a major part of housekeeping becomes shifting these items around in order to create enough space to work in any given area. "Imagine," said Lucid, "living in the house that you now live in, and you haven't thrown anything away for over ten years, and then you bring in some new things. Well, where are you going to put it?"[31]

Resupply

All the necessities of life must be brought to the station from Earth on a regular basis. This is done on supply ships—either a space shuttle or a robotic cargo ship called Progress. A Progress ship, flying on autopilot, arrives every few weeks and docks with the space station. The astronauts on board the station can see it approach, closing the distance between them with every orbit of Earth. Finally it appears right outside the window, its docking lights shining brightly and its solar panels outstretched like a pair of arms. The astronauts can see the braking thrusters fire at regular intervals, appearing simultaneously as silent puffs of gas on two sides of the spacecraft (to keep the ship stable). When the Progress docks, the station rocks noticeably. Computer monitors sway on their mountings, and the ventilation tubes that run throughout the station flex back and forth. The vibrations gradually diminish as the station absorbs the gentle impact of the docking.

After the astronauts determine that there is a proper seal between the Progress and the space station, they open the space station's hatch. Immediately they smell a distinct odor that astronauts have come to associate with space itself. Although scientists do not know for certain what causes this smell, some astronauts have described it as similar to the smell of cold ashes in a fireplace. Finally, the astronauts open the hatch of the Progress and are treated to the smells of Earth, including fresh food such as apples and lemons.

The Soyuz is a basic, no-frills spacecraft, but the Progress, the cargo version of the Soyuz, is even more stripped down, as Valentin Lebedev, an astronaut aboard the Russian *Salyut-7* space station, explained:

> It doesn't have a life-support system: there is only one fan and one light bulb. Many particles float there because it is difficult to remove them completely on the ground. During the dismounting of the equipment [sent to the station aboard Progress] a lot of metal dust comes out. . . . Inside the resupply ship compartment are the odors of lacquers, glue, rubber, and metal.[32]

The Progress ship contains fresh food, water, clothing, fuel for the station's attitude control thrusters, replacement parts, and equipment for scientific experiments. The Progress also contains packages of letters, photos, and presents from family members and friends back on Earth. Called "psychological support packages" by NASA, these are among the most treasured items on the Progress, and the astronauts dig through the other cargo to unpack them first.

A Progress cargo vehicle approaches a space station with supplies and news from home. The station's crew eagerly anticipates its arrival.

Free Time

As important to the astronauts' mental health as the personal items sent from home is their free time. Space station residents get time off from work and chores on weekends, just as they do on Earth. The ways in which the astronauts pass their free time are as individual as the astronauts themselves, but they agree on one thing, as Carr explained: "The number-one form of entertainment on the space station is looking out the window and taking pictures of things that you recognize. We observed things like hurricanes and dust storms, forest fires, volcanoes spewing."[33]

In addition to looking out the window, astronauts on space stations spend their free time watching movies, reading books, playing and

Watching the World Go By

The view of Earth from a space station changes constantly. Over a period of weeks, the astronauts can observe seasonal changes—lakes freezing over, the land turning brown, and then turning green again in spring. When the station's orbit takes it over the night side of Earth, the astronauts can see the lights of cities and the flashes of lightning storms high up in the atmosphere.

In his book *Diary of a Cosmonaut*, Valentin Lebedev described watching another type of spectacular natural light show while aboard *Salyut-7:*

"I watched the Aurora Australis in the Southern Hemisphere above Antarctica. This really is the end of the world! Magnificent! Light-colored cloud wreaths spread on the horizon, fountains of white-green-burgundy streams reaching up to the stars, surrounding the station as we flew in Earth's shadow through the light jungles of silent space."

The natural light shows of the auroras are just one of the spectacular views space station residents enjoy from their seat above the world.

listening to music, and talking with friends and family back home via satellite and radio link. They also enjoy reading mail from home and talking with ham (amateur) radio operators who contact them as they pass overhead.

The astronauts usually have an hour or two before bedtime to read, write letters home, or just float quietly. Linenger described how meaningful it was for him to write letters home to his son at the end of the day:

> At the end of the day, I would float over to a laptop computer and start talking with my boy through the writing of letters.

Sometimes I would find myself uplifted by my reminiscences of him; other times I would find tears welling up in my eyes from missing him. The letter writing became a therapy of sorts for me, a time to reflect on the day's events and unwind by talking with my son. Letter complete, usually around midnight, I would fly over to the wall that I slept on and fall asleep.[34]

Getting Ready for Bed

Further contributing to a homey feeling aboard a space station are the astronauts' schedules and routines, which closely mirror those the astronauts follow on Earth. For instance, before bed (and after getting up in the morning) the astronauts brush their teeth using a toothbrush and toothpaste, much as they would on Earth—with a difference. Linenger explained:

> I can brush my teeth pretty well as long as I keep my mouth closed. If I open my mouth and breathe out just a bit, the toothpaste foam starts to float away. I keep a small two-by-two gauze pad nearby and carefully capture the stuff in it. Then, I transfer the dampened gauze to a plastic Ziploc bag, remembering to seal it tightly.[35]

After space station astronauts have finished brushing their teeth, they spit the remaining toothpaste into a towel.

Hitting the Sack

Sleeping, too, is very different than on Earth. Instead of climbing into a bed, astronauts strap themselves into sleeping bags at the end of the day, and then either tether themselves to a space station wall or allow themselves to drift within their sleeping compartments. Some astronauts find that floating while sleeping is disconcerting, so they are more comfortable if they strap themselves to the wall with bungee cords. The pressure of the cords against their bodies provides an approximation of the sensation of lying on a bed on Earth.

An astronaut smiles from his cramped sleeping compartment aboard the ISS. Some astronauts find weightless sleeping very restful.

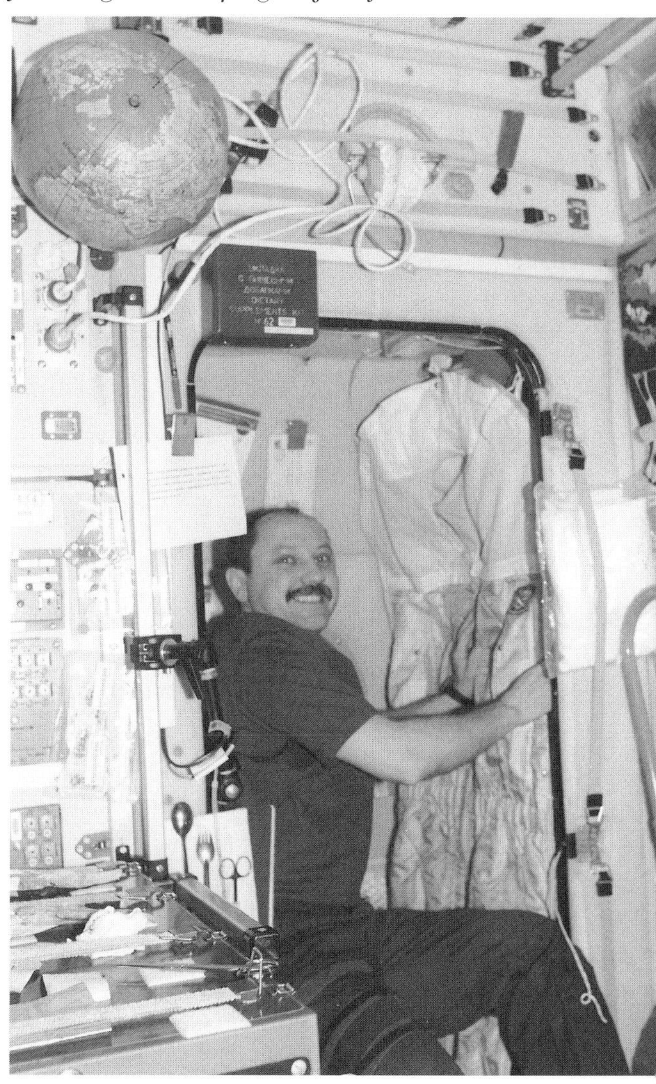

Some astronauts have their own closet-sized sleeping compartments, complete with a porthole that allows them to watch Earth and the stars before they drift off to sleep. Others simply unfurl their sleeping bags in a clear area of the station, tie up to a nearby handle so they don't drift too far, cover up any nearby windows, and then turn out the lights to sleep.

On Earth, the heated air of a sleeper's exhalations rises, carrying carbon dioxide away from the sleeper's face. Because heated air neither rises nor falls in a weightless environment, carbon dioxide tends to build up around astronauts' heads as they sleep. For this reason, astronauts without a sleeping compartment make sure that they sleep in a place where they can feel a breeze from a ventilation fan blowing over their heads. "Without air movement," wrote Linenger, "we will find ourselves enclosed within a self-generated carbon dioxide bubble, waking up panting for air. More likely than not, the air hunger is accompanied by a headache."[36]

Many astronauts have found that sleeping weightless is more restful than sleeping in a bed on Earth; there is no soreness from sleeping on a lumpy mattress, and any position is comfortable. "Sleeping on board is fun," Lebedev wrote from *Salyut-7*. "You can sleep here in any position: standing, upside down, or on a ceiling. Since you don't feel any gravity, even if you lie on one side the whole night long, your side won't go to sleep. You sleep without tossing and turning."[37]

Eating, using the toilet, bathing, sleeping, and having fun all present unique challenges and pleasures to astronauts living aboard a space station. Although a space station is in many ways very much like a terrestrial home, the astronauts find reminders at every turn that they are hundreds of miles from the surface of Earth and far from their ordinary lives. These reminders come to the astronauts not only as they get up in the morning, eat, and sleep, but also while they conduct the work they were sent to the station to do.

CHAPTER 4

Working in Space

People living aboard space stations are called upon to perform a wide variety of tasks, including conducting scientific experiments impossible to perform on Earth, installing new space station modules and components, and even shooting television commercials and conducting other public relations work. Because space stations can support only a few people at a time, everyone aboard must learn aspects of all the jobs that need to be done. Scientists, construction workers, photographers, filmmakers, and even actors—space station residents can claim to be all of these and more.

Science in Orbit

The unique conditions aboard a space station—weightlessness among them—make it an ideal place to carry out certain scientific experiments. These experiments include growing plants and tending to laboratory animals to see how these organisms behave in weightlessness.

Astronauts also conduct experiments on themselves and measure their own physiological adaptation to weightlessness. Station inhabitants conduct other experiments in the area of materials science, creating crystals and other materials that would be impossible to produce on Earth. They also make astronomical observations unimpeded by the atmospheric distortion that hinders ground-based observatories.

Many of the experiments on board a space station would be disturbed by even the very small effects of acceleration such as those produced by the firing of thrusters to change the station's position, or attitude, in order to keep the solar panels pointed at the sun. For this reason, these especially delicate experiments are housed in a special rack. Although the rack is firmly secured to a wall, it is known as the floating rack because it uses shock absorbers to isolate the experiments from jolts, no matter how slight.

Human Guinea Pigs

One of the most important functions of a space station is to study the effects of long-duration space flight on the human body. During space voyages, muscles atrophy and bones lose calcium. This is because in weightless conditions muscles and bones do not have to keep the body upright, so they weaken. The heart, too, weakens because it does not have to pump blood against the pull of gravity. For this reason, much of the work astronauts do on a space station involves conducting experiments to measure the effects of weightlessness on the human body and trying to develop ways to counteract these effects. Some experiments keep track of the changes in muscle mass and bone density. For instance, astronauts measure their body mass by strapping themselves to a device that vibrates and measures

Farmers in the Sky

Astronauts on long voyages to other planets, during which they will have to remain in space for many months or even years, will not be able to be resupplied by cargo ships from Earth. For that reason, one of the most important biology experiments aboard space stations has been to try to grow the kinds of food crops that outward-bound space voyagers might take with them. Wheat, peas, onions, and oats have all been grown aboard space stations, with varying degrees of success.

But if a plant fails to thrive aboard a space station, it is not for lack of care. Astronauts lovingly tend their little farms in space. The plants are the only greenery in the small world of the space station, and for that reason, they are precious. Valentin Lebedev described the small, glass-enclosed terrarium on board *Salyut-7* in his *Diary of a Cosmonaut.*

"The pea and oat plants are growing behind my sleeping bag; behind the panel in the Oazis is our farm. The stems are in bud with leaves like small bluebells, still weak, but fresh and green. They make me happy; they were born in space."

An ISS science officer proudly displays his pea plant terrarium. Green, living plants are precious commodities aboard the station.

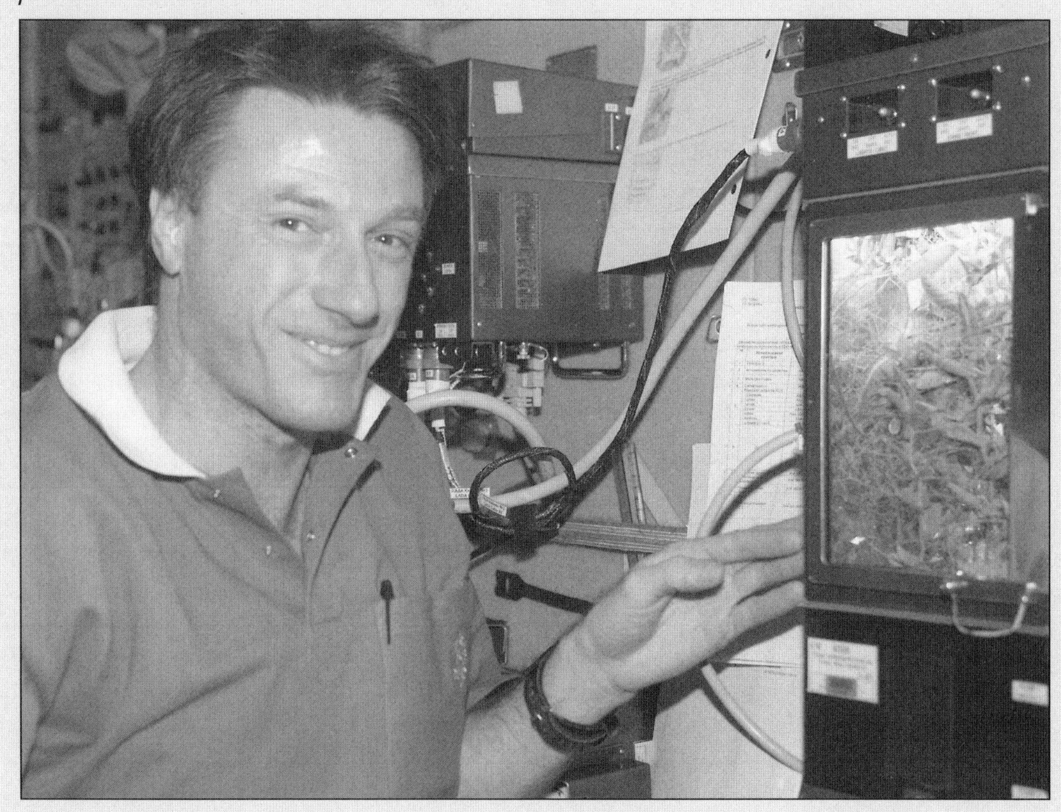

the resulting counter vibrations to calculate mass.

In addition, at various times during their stay on board a space station, astronauts draw their blood for later analysis on Earth, or give themselves or each other injections to test the effectiveness of various medicines in space. They also use medical sensors to record their heart rate, blood pressure, respiration, and other vital signs at regular intervals. These data are transmitted to mission control in real time so that doctors and scientists on Earth can track changes over time. These experiments are not the most pleasant aspect of an astronaut's workday, as Lebedev explained:

> These occasions don't excite us very much. In order to do medical experiments, we have to unpack all the medical cartridges with sensors, cuffs, and medical belts, tubes with paste, and napkins. Then, depending on the instructions, we have to attach different electrodes and sensors to our bodies, adjust them, and try to get a good display of readings on the screen. We have to sit naked, hooked up to all those electrodes and sensors, among cables and wires, which float like seaweed. . . .[38]

While attached to the medical sensors, the astronauts may also be required to use the onboard exercise equipment, such as the stationary bicycle and the treadmill, so that the doctors and scientists on the ground can keep track of the changes in the astronauts' vital signs under various levels of physical exertion. The astronauts may also put on gas masks designed to precisely analyze the composition of their exhalations, including carbon dioxide concentrations. An ultrasound machine may also be used to examine physical changes in the astronauts' internal organs, such as changes in the size of the heart, caused by weightlessness.

Large geographical features like fault zones are easier to see from a space station.

Astronomy and Earth Science

Because the space station is situated outside the distorting effects of Earth's atmosphere, it is an ideal place to make observations of the sun, the planets, and the rest of the universe, using telescopes and cameras. For instance, their remove from atmospheric distortion allows the astronauts to observe activity on the surface of the sun, including solar flares and sunspots, with much greater clarity than can be done from Earth. In addition to observing the sun and other celestial bodies in the visible wavelengths, as with conventional telescopes, the astronauts make observations with

From the vantage point of space, astronauts can study features on earth like the snow pattern on Japan's Mt. Fuji or events like the eruption of Mt. Etna in Italy (inset).

telescopes that allow them to see wavelengths not visible to the naked eye, including X-rays, microwaves, and infrared and ultraviolet light.

Orbiting the Earth two hundred miles up also gives astronauts a unique vantage point from which to study Earth's surface. From their orbiting observatory, the astronauts can track air and water pollution patterns, the global distribution of various types of crops, and seasonal changes to waterways and ground cover.

Astronauts on a space station can also observe geological and oceanographic features that are too big to be seen in their entirety on the surface, such as earthquake fault zones and ocean currents. Astronauts can also document changes in bodies of water over time. Carr described one set of observations he made as part of *Skylab*'s earth science program:

> We were up there from November into February so we took periodic photographs

of the St. Lawrence Seaway as it was freezing over. That was really an interesting little program to watch how that worked. The water would freeze with a thin layer of ice and then the wind would come up and blow the ice to one shore or the other. When the wind died down, water would freeze again and then the wind would come up and push it to one shore or the other, and we just saw gradually this big crusty shoreline moving toward the middle until it froze over.[39]

Materials Science

The weightless environment aboard a space station makes it possible to create materials that cannot be duplicated on Earth. Weightlessness allows astronauts to grow both organic and inorganic crystalline structures for use in medicines and as semiconductors, and to create alloys and other industrial products with unsurpassed purity. These materials develop flaws when created in Earth's gravity because heavier elements sink to the bottom of alloys as they cool, and because the materials come into contact with the containers in which they are formed. Not so in space.

Many scientific experiments aboard a space station involve the creation of new materials and medicines in miniature factories for later analysis on Earth. Although it is currently too expensive to create these materials in commercially useful quantities in space, engineers hope these experiments can someday be expanded into the large-scale manufacture of such materials in Earth orbit. For now, the experiments help scientists and engineers improve their manufacturing processes on Earth.

Because many of the substances used in these experiments are toxic, they present a particular hazard in the station's closed environment. Therefore, astronauts conduct the experiments in a sealed "glovebox." By fitting

A space station science officer uses the sealed glovebox to safely conduct experiments. Zero gravity conditions allow for creation of unique materials.

their hands into the gloves, which protrude into the glovebox, astronauts can manipulate potentially dangerous substances, watching the results of the experiments through the box's window. This way poisonous vapors and other hazardous by-products of the experiments are prevented from fouling the station's atmosphere and can be disposed of properly.

Other experiments involve exposing different industrial materials to the vacuum, cosmic radiation, and micrometeorites outside the space station. Space-walking astronauts attach specially designed trays to the hull of the station and then retrieve them after a set period of time. The trays are then returned to Earth so that the effects of space on various materials can be studied by scientists.

Hard Hats in Space

A major part of the work aboard a space station involves ongoing construction and major maintenance work. When new space station modules arrive from Earth, they must be at-

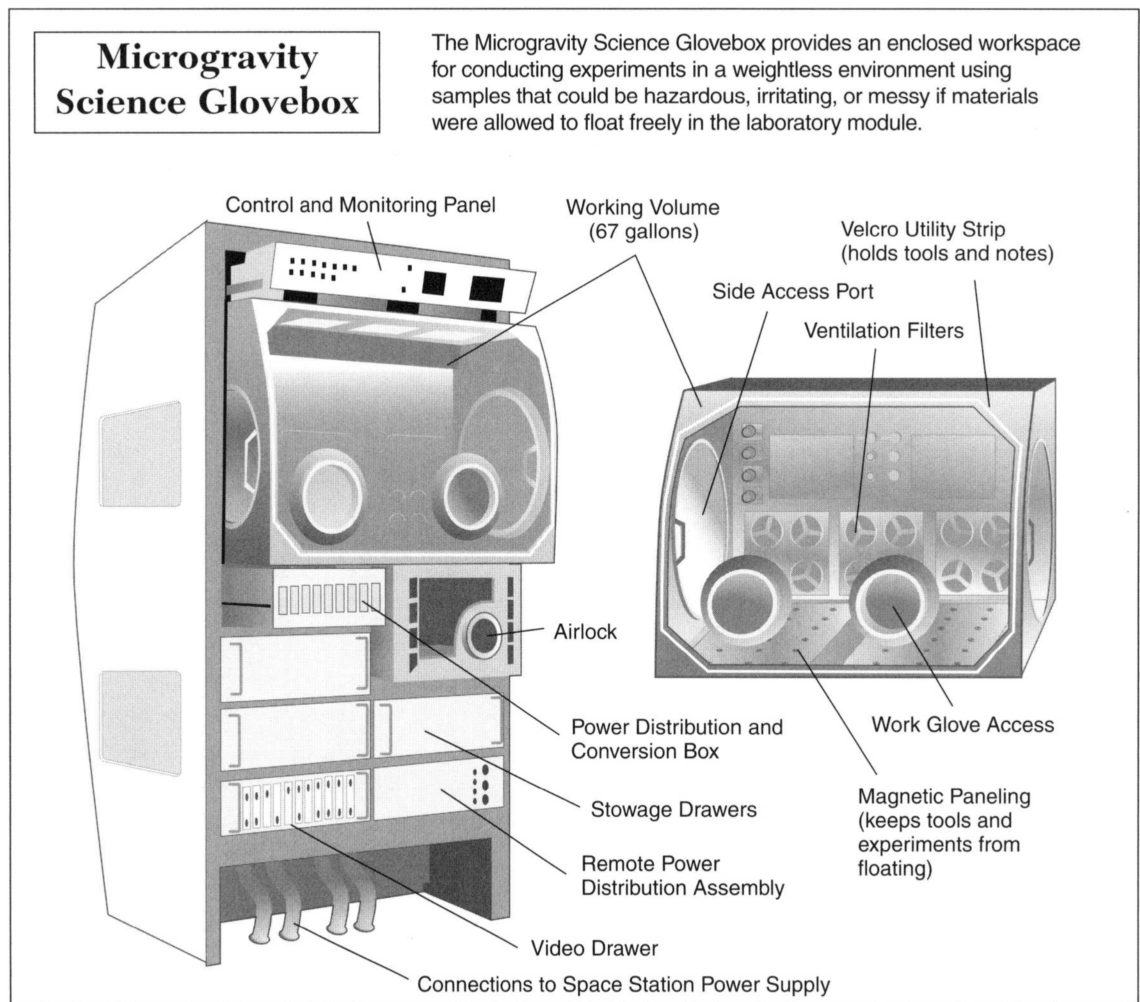

Source: NASA Microgravity Science and Applications Department (http://msad.msfc.nasa.gov).

tached to the existing station components. Solar panels on the new modules must be unfurled, and other components must be attached to the modules' exteriors. Much of this work requires spacewalking, or extravehicular activity (EVA).

A new space station module is sent up from Earth either on a space shuttle or on its own booster rocket. A module sent by a space shuttle travels in the shuttle's cargo bay. The new module is carefully docked to the rest of the station by the shuttle crew using the shuttle's robot arm. A module that is sent up to the station by itself flies as an independent spacecraft to the station, where it docks on automatic pilot.

Following the docking, the new module must be fully connected to the station. Space-suited astronauts working outside the station connect the electrical systems, cooling systems, and other systems by means of cables. As each end of a cable is attached, either to the new module or to the rest of the station, it is locked firmly into place and protected with thermal insulation. The space walkers may also be called upon to unfurl antennas and attach solar panels to the outside of the station. Space stations draw their power from the sun using the solar panels, and each new module increases the energy demands of the station, requiring the addition of new panels.

After the new module is attached to the station and their systems are connected, astronauts inside the station can finally open the hatches and expand their living space. But things do not always go as planned. Lucid described some problems related to opening a new module for space station *Mir:*

> When Priroda [the new module] came, while it was in progress, there was a fire inside that the ground had picked up. So after it docked, we weren't allowed to open it for a while till the ground figured out what to do; we had to figure out that the atmosphere was okay in Priroda before we could open it up. So then they finally agreed that we could open up the hatch and we opened it up and there was a little bit of smoke debris and there was debris from leaking batteries in there that we had to clean up before we could get Priroda up and running.[40]

Stepping Out

When an astronaut's work requires going outside the space station, getting into a space suit is a painstaking and time-consuming process. Nothing can be left to chance; one improperly closed seal can result in loss of air pressure inside the suit, which in the vacuum of space would be fatal.

To prepare for an EVA, astronauts must first ready the station's airlock and their space suits. The airlock is often used for storage between space walks, so all the equipment and other items that have been stored there must be removed. Then the astronauts take their suits out of their storage places in the airlock. They check to make sure that the suits' oxygen tanks are filled with oxygen, that the cooling systems are filled with water, and that the batteries, which power the suits' radios, headlamps, life support systems, and other equipment, are fully charged. The space suits' cooling water evaporates while the suits are in storage, so it is important to make sure that there is enough remaining for an EVA.

Next, the astronauts spend time breathing pure oxygen from masks while exercising on a stationary bicycle or other exercise machine.

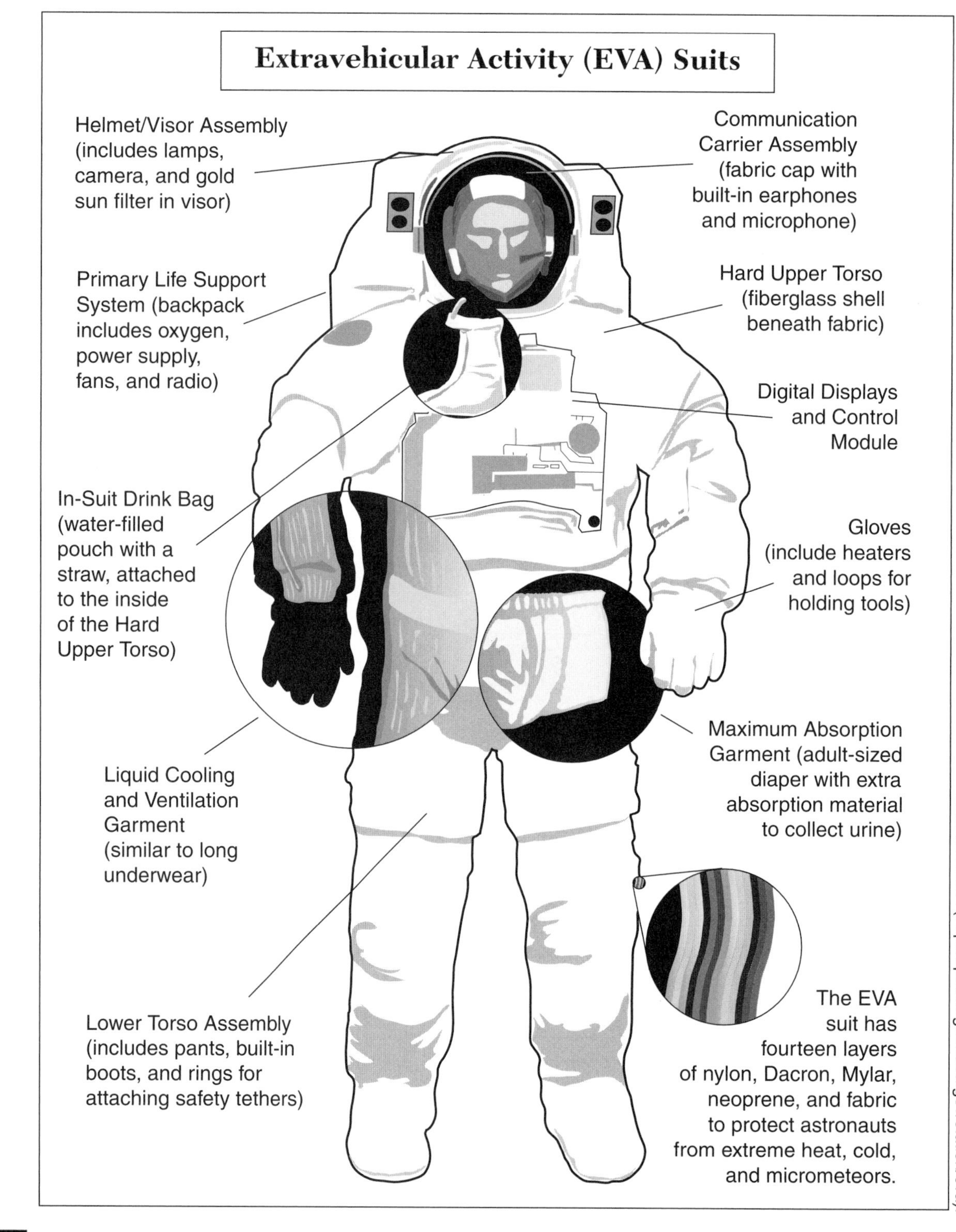
Extravehicular Activity (EVA) Suits
Helmet/Visor Assembly (includes lamps, camera, and gold sun filter in visor)
Communication Carrier Assembly (fabric cap with built-in earphones and microphone)
Primary Life Support System (backpack includes oxygen, power supply, fans, and radio)
Hard Upper Torso (fiberglass shell beneath fabric)
Digital Displays and Control Module
In-Suit Drink Bag (water-filled pouch with a straw, attached to the inside of the Hard Upper Torso)
Gloves (include heaters and loops for holding tools)
Maximum Absorption Garment (adult-sized diaper with extra absorption material to collect urine)
Liquid Cooling and Ventilation Garment (similar to long underwear)
Lower Torso Assembly (includes pants, built-in boots, and rings for attaching safety tethers)
The EVA suit has fourteen layers of nylon, Dacron, Mylar, neoprene, and fabric to protect astronauts from extreme heat, cold, and micrometeors.
Source: NASA (http://spaceflight.nasa.gov/station/eva).

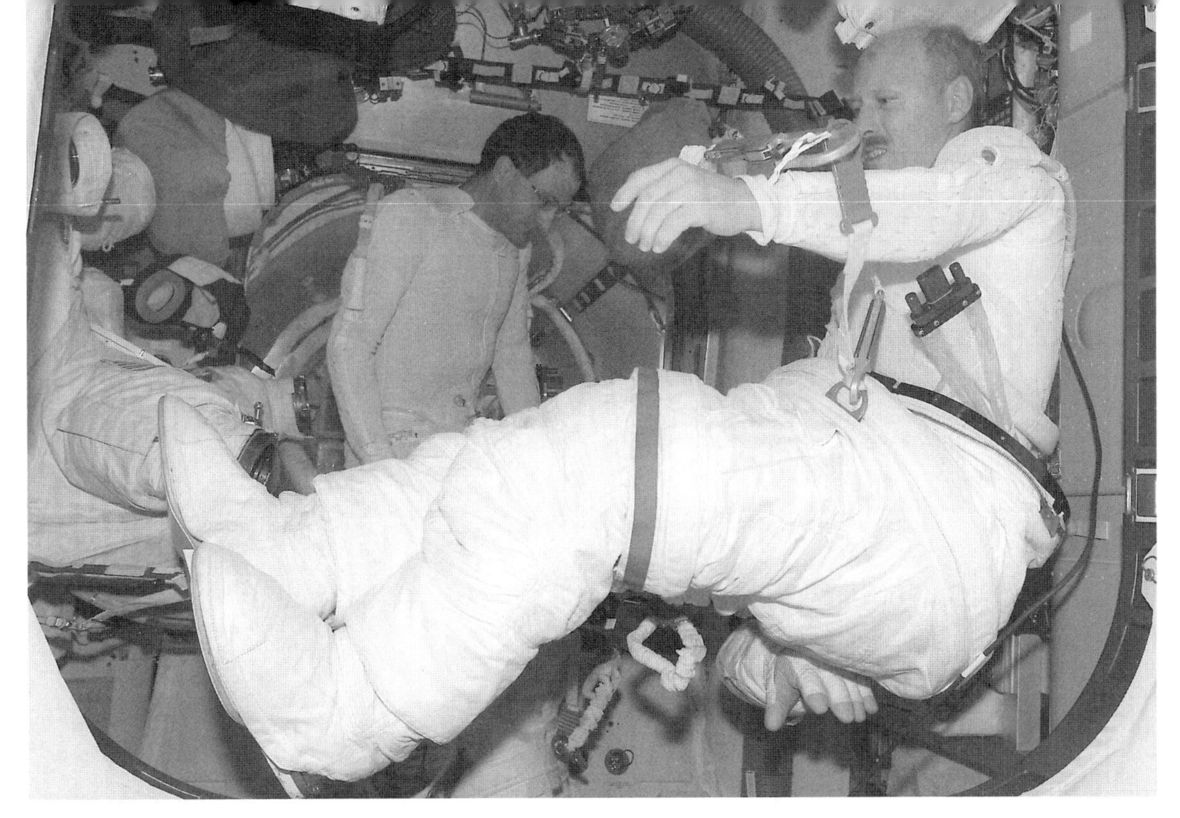

Going outside a station necessitates wearing a pressurized suit. Here, astronauts about to exit the ISS struggle to don the heavy suits in zero gravity.

This purges their blood of nitrogen—a must because the internal pressure of the space suits is lower than that of the space station environment. This lower pressure would cause nitrogen in the blood to form bubbles, leading to decompression sickness, also known as the bends.

Finally, the astronauts help each other into their space suits, seal them up, and then check them for leaks. Then—and only then—can they close the inner door of the airlock, pump out the air, and open the door to outer space.

On Top of the World

Lebedev compared opening the hatch to go outside of *Salyut-7* to opening "the door of a log cabin on a sunny, cold day" and flooding it with brilliant sunshine: "Tiny glitterlike dust flew away from the station. Space, the gigantic vacuum cleaner, began to suck everything out of the [airlock of the] station. Small bolts and screws, lost long ago, drifted along with the dust from behind the compartment wall quilting; a pencil drifted out too."[41] When spacewalking at night, said astronaut Kenneth Bowersox, "You can see city lights, you can see lightning. If there's moon glow, you can see some color from the continents and reflections off the ocean. . . ."[42] In general, he said,

> the view is much more captivating outside than through the space station windows because it's so wide. Through the window you always have a limit to your view and you feel like you're looking through a window. The helmet on your space suit, it's really just a

window, but it's got a wider panorama, and there's less glass between you and what's outside, so the colors are . . . more vivid.[43]

Linenger had a less-than-peaceful experience during an EVA. He likened walking on the outside of space station *Mir* to moving along the face of a cliff that was falling through empty space, taking him along with it; stopping work to enjoy the view was not uppermost on his mind.

Wing Walkers in Space

Space-walking astronauts, working in pairs for safety's sake, stay firmly attached to the station with lifelines that prevent them from flying off

While outside the station, this astronaut must be secured with a lifeline lest he drift off into space. Some crewmembers find such spacewalks thrilling.

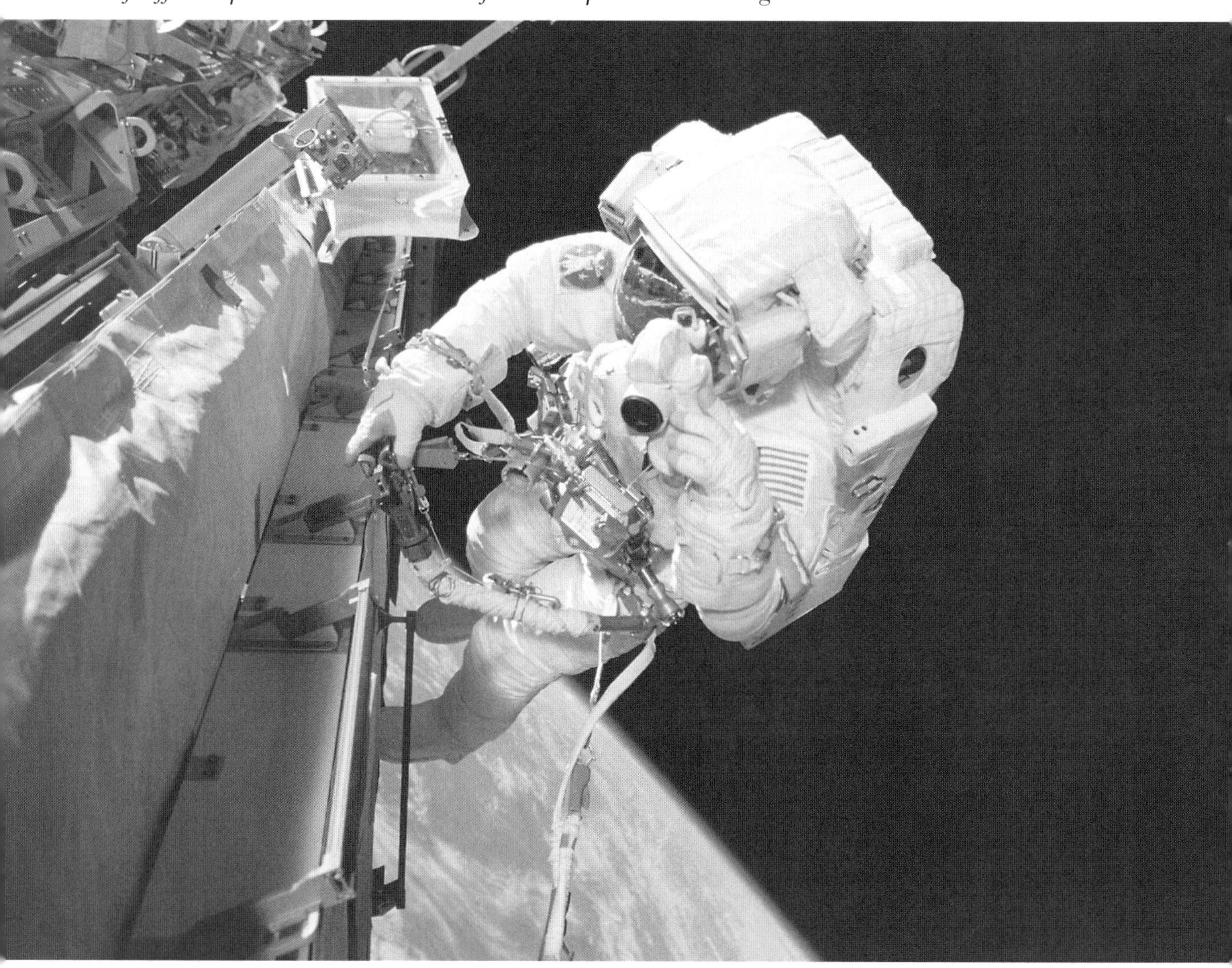

into space. Without the lifelines, an astronaut who let go of the handholds on the station's hull could easily drift away from the station. It would be very difficult to retrieve a drifting astronaut because the station cannot easily maneuver to pick him or her up. For this reason, in addition to their lifelines, space-walking astronauts wear emergency jetpacks called Simplified Aid for EVA Rescue, or SAFER. The SAFER allows a drifting astronaut to jet back to handholds on the station's hull. From there, he or she can spacewalk, hand over hand, to the safety of an airlock.

For many astronauts, a space walk is the high point of their careers. Carr described the most memorable moment of one of his space walks on *Skylab:*

> I remember going up on the very top of the spacecraft where the Apollo Telescope Mount was located and fastening my feet into the foot restraints and then standing up and looking away from the spacecraft. See, we were upside down at that time and I was looking at the earth by looking up and couldn't see any of the spacecraft around me. Flying along, I felt like a wing walker, like one of those old barnstorming wing walkers [daredevils who would walk on the wings of slow-moving airplanes in flight]. . . . It was just a wonderful experience. Just me and the earth.[44]

Repair and Maintenance

Keeping a space station in good working order is often the reason for a space walk, but even if this work does not involve going outside, a space suit may be required. For instance, if a module is punctured, perhaps by a collision with a spacecraft, the astronauts will have to suit up before they can go inside and patch the leaks.

However, much of the ongoing maintenance and repair work required of station residents can be done from the inside, without space suits. A space station is full of electrical and mechanical components that can break down at any time. Since there is no way to return the station to Earth for service, it is up to the astronauts to either make their own repairs or cope with broken equipment as best they can. Lucid explained:

> Toward the end of the flight, we spent a lot of time wiping up water because we were having problems with the cooling loops, etc., and so there was a lot of condensate that was showing up inside the different modules. We spent a lot of time jerry-rigging various things to either soak up the water or suck it up.[45]

Public Relations

The astronauts' duties often require not only technical expertise, but also a knack for public relations. Space station crews are often called upon to participate in live interviews with journalists, students, or other members of the general public. This is necessary because most of the funding for spaceflights and for the operation of space stations comes from governments whose leaders must demonstrate to their citizens the value of using public funds for space missions.

Newcomers to a station usually have a video news conference scheduled for immediately after their arrival. From then on, news conferences and interviews with journalists on Earth become a regular part of work life on the station throughout their stay. Astronauts

The Jet Set

One of the mainstays of science fiction about space travel is the jetpack that allows astronauts to fly independent of a spacecraft. The space station *Skylab* was the proving ground for just such a jetpack, called the astronaut maneuvering unit. Because the interior of *Skylab* was so spacious, astronauts on board could test the jetpack inside, without having to put on space suits first. *Skylab* commander Gerry Carr described the maneuvering unit to the author:

"It was like a great big overstuffed chair you were fastened into, and it had thruster jets and nitrogen tanks for the fuel. It had a very, very sophisticated gyro system in it that kept it stabilized and made it very, very easy to move around and do very accurate work. It was an interesting way to move around. It was kind of like being on an elevator, but the elevator went three different directions instead of just one."

Because the maneuvering unit used nitrogen gas for propulsion, the astronauts aboard *Skylab* had to pump extra oxygen into the station's atmosphere before they rode their onboard flying machine. When they were finished testing the maneuvering unit, they had to pump the excess nitrogen back out of the station's atmosphere.

might also shoot film footage of each other and their lives aboard the station for documentaries and television programs.

Space station inhabitants sometimes even shoot video footage for use in television commercials for corporations that want to use the unique environment of a space station to distinguish their products from others; products used by astronauts in space have carried a cachet as being particularly innovative and durable since the early days of space exploration. Although NASA has been reluctant to allow its astronauts and equipment to be used in the promotion of products, the RSA has no such qualms.

Russian astronauts and space station components have been used in commercials for soft drinks, fast food, space pens, and retailers. As part of a publicity campaign for a pizza chain in 2001, Russian astronauts delivered a specially created pizza to the International Space Station, where it was baked in the station's oven and eaten with fanfare by the astronauts. In 1996, space-walking astronauts on *Mir* brought a four-foot-tall inflatable replica of a soft drink container outside with them to use in shooting a Pepsi commercial.

Space Tourism

Just as NASA has been reluctant to associate itself with commercial messages, the agency has tried to keep its space station programs from the possible distractions of other nonscientific uses, such as space tourism. Therefore, as with advertising in space, the RSA has taken the lead in bringing paying passengers into space stations.

Wealthy American businessman Dennis Tito became the first person to pay his own way to a space station in 2001, when he traveled to the International Space Station aboard a Soyuz spacecraft. He was followed the next year by South African space tourist Mark Shuttleworth, who was also flown to the station by the RSA. Each of these space tourists stayed aboard the International Space Station about a week, and each paid $20 million for the vacation of a lifetime.

Besides the rigorous screening and training all astronauts must undergo before traveling to a space station, space tourists also have to pay a fortune for the privilege, so they plan their activities as carefully as their professional colleagues. Tito spent much of his time on board the International Space Station gazing out the windows at Earth while listening to opera music. He also took many photographs, and assisted the rest of the crew in food preparation and other simple tasks so that they could spend more of their time performing their other duties.

As if the jobs of scientist, research subject, public relations specialist, and construction worker were not enough, space station crew members must add one more job description to their list of duties—emergency worker.

CHAPTER 5

Handling Emergencies

Danger on a space station is never farther away than the nearly perfect vacuum on the other side of a thin metal wall. Station inhabitants must be prepared for a wide range of emergencies, from fire to life support and power failures to decompression. Within the closed environment of a space station, emergencies tend to multiply. Fires can overload life support equipment with smoke, collisions can cause decompression and loss of power, and so on. Even an illness or injury that would be considered minor on Earth, where the victim can easily get to a doctor or hospital, might be considered an emergency on board a space station.

Emergencies can strike at any time. Space station crews cannot depend on any help from Earth reaching them in time if there is an emergency on board. Even if there were a rescue ship ready to launch from Earth—a very unlikely possibility—in the two days required to reach the station, an emergency would have run its course, with potentially lethal consequences. The station crew must therefore be prepared to react quickly and decisively if an emergency strikes. And in case the emergency cannot be overcome, the crew must be prepared to evacuate the station on short notice.

Fire

Fire is one of the most serious emergencies that can strike a space station, and it is a constant danger. There are many possible ways for a fire to start. Electrical short circuits, overheated equipment, and out-of-control experiments all have the potential to set off a fire aboard a space station. A station crew must react quickly if a fire breaks out. A fire can spread swiftly through the station's ventilation system. Smoke can also be circulated by the ventilation system, quickly fouling the station's air.

Should a fire break out, the astronauts must shut down the ventilation system, don oxygen masks, and combat the fire with special fire extinguishers that use either carbon dioxide or a combination of foam and water to smother the blaze, or at the very least stop it from spreading further until it burns out on its own. Should all else fail and they cannot stop the fire from spreading, the astronauts must climb into the attached escape capsule and flee. Doing so would mean the certain destruction of the station, so this is a last resort.

A Desperate Situation

Six astronauts aboard the space station *Mir* faced a fire early in 1997. Although the normal complement of *Mir* was only three people, up to six astronauts stayed at the station during crew exchanges, which lasted twenty days or so. The changeover period on a space station is a festive occasion, as departing crew members greet new faces after months of looking only at each other, and their thoughts turn toward their homes and families soon to be rejoined back on Earth.

Because *Mir* was designed to support only three people for extended periods of time, the normal life support system had to be supplemented by a backup oxygen-generating system when more people were aboard. The backup system consisted of special oxygen "candles," canisters of potassium perchlorate that released oxygen when heated.

The six astronauts had gathered in celebration around the dining table in *Mir*'s Base Block, the control module, eating caviar and fresh lemons from Earth. Astronaut Sasha Lazutkin left the table to change a depleted oxygen candle. It was later determined that the new canister had a leak that allowed flammable gases to escape when Lazutkin activated

These astronauts don breathing masks to train for an emergency in space. Fire aboard a space station is always a danger and did occur in 1997.

Fighting Fires in Space

Fires are a constant danger aboard space stations, and finding more effective ways of fighting them is the subject of many of the experiments conducted in space. As part of some of the experiments conducted aboard the station, fires are lit under controlled conditions in sealed containers. Various materials are ignited, and the behavior of the flames is recorded both on videotape and through the written and verbal observations of the astronauts conducting the experiments. In addition to observing the behavior of flames, the astronauts also observe the behavior of smoldering materials in order to gather data on the behavior of fires that might start out of sight, for instance, behind electrical panels.

In the absence of gravity, flames do not rise; rather, they spread out in a ball around the source of the flame. This means that, left to itself, a fire will not spread as rapidly in an enclosed space as it will in a similar space on Earth. However, a space station's ventilation system is designed to circulate oxygen throughout the station, and this can help spread a fire very rapidly. For this reason, the station's ventilation system is designed to be shut off if a fire is detected.

Smoke detectors are used to alert crew members to a fire before it becomes serious, just as they are on Earth. On Earth, smoke detectors are placed on the ceiling because smoke from a fire rises. However, since smoke does not rise on a space station, the smoke detectors are placed in the ventilation system, as this is where the smoke, along with everything else in the station's air supply, will eventually be drawn.

the canister. The results, recalled astronaut Jerry Linenger, were disastrous:

> I looked down the passageway and I could see a very large flame bursting out of the canister, smoke billowing out, and I knew we had a big problem. Molten metal was flying across, splattering on the other bulkhead, which meant it was hot. The flame was at least . . . two, three feet, directional. It had oxygen, it had fuel, had everything it needed.[46]

The Base Block quickly began to fill with smoke. Lazutkin described his feelings at the time:

> When I saw the ship was full of smoke, my natural earthly reaction was to want to open a window. And then I was truly afraid for the first time. You're in such a small space that you can't escape. . . . You can't just open a window to ventilate the room.[47]

Quick Action Saves a Crew

With no way to clear the room of smoke, the astronauts had to immediately put on emergency oxygen masks and get fresh air before they succumbed to smoke inhalation. They then had to act just as quickly to put out the fire. If the fire could not be prevented from spreading, at least three of *Mir*'s crew members would be killed. There were two escape ships attached to the station at the time, but access to one of them was blocked by the fire. Since the accessible ship could hold only three people, escape was not an option.

Mir's commander, Valeri Korzun, attacked the blaze with a fire extinguisher, but the equipment, designed on Earth and untested in space, did not function as planned. Instead of settling on the flames as it would have on Earth, the extinguisher's foam floated away and the blaze continued unabated. Fortunately the extinguisher had another mode that allowed it to spray water instead of foam, and Korzun used that instead. The water helped to keep the fire from spreading by getting surrounding flammable materials wet. Korzun discharged the contents of two more extinguishers on the flames, and the fire finally died after consuming its fuel.

The crew's quick response to the fire prevented it from causing any real damage, and the air filtration system, along with the simple action of smoke-laden, free-floating water from the fire extinguishers condensing on the station's cold walls, soon removed the smoke from the air.

Decompression

As fearsome as the prospect of fire is, the sensation space station crews most dread is the feeling of their ears popping due to a drop in air pressure, for this means that the station is in danger of decompression from a breach in the hull. This can happen if the station is struck and punctured by another orbiting object, such as an out-of-control spacecraft. Exactly this event occurred on *Mir* just a few weeks after the fire, when a test of a new manual-docking procedure went awry. Lazutkin watched from *Mir* as the Progress cargo ship undergoing testing crashed into the station instead of docking:

> It was full of menace, like a shark. I watched this black body covered with spots sliding past below me. I looked closer, and at that point, there was a great thump, and the whole station shook.[48]

The station's decompression alarms began to blare; the astronauts had to work quickly to either stop the leak of oxygen into space or escape from the station.

Isolating a Leak

Each section, or module, of a space station is separated from the others by an airtight hatch. This makes it possible to seal off a leaking module from the others before the entire station decompresses. Before they start the process of sealing off the damaged module, however, the astronauts prepare the escape ship for immediate departure; if all else fails, the crew will have one more chance to preserve their lives.

It takes only a few seconds to prepare the escape ship, and then the crew members quickly turn their attention to isolating the leak. This may be easier said than done; in order to close the hatch to the leaking module, the crew may first have to disconnect power, communications, and other cables that may be running through the damaged module's hatchway. This was the case after the collision on *Mir*. Foale described some of the difficulties he and Lazutkin faced as they worked to seal the leaking Spektr module:

> We got to one thin cable that had no obvious plug on either side, and it was the last one left that was stopping us from closing the hatch. And Sasha says, "Is there a knife?" And I looked around and there was no knife apparent in the node [the spherical module that connected several *Mir* modules, including Spektr]. Sasha had to go and get one from the kitchen table, and he brought back a kitchen knife and started sawing on this. And we got sparks coming out of it. So I said, "Sasha, I don't think we should try and saw this, this is too bad."[49]

ISS crewmembers practice an evacuation drill on board. Their first duty is to ready the escape vehicles.

After the astronauts clear all the obstacles from the hatchway, as Foale and Lazutkin were finally able to do, they may still find it impossible to close the hatch if the hatch is located inside the damaged module. The river of air rushing through the station and out through the puncture in the module may prove too great a force to pull the hatch against. In this case, the astronauts may have to place a spare hatch cover over the hatchway, where the air pressure will work in their favor to seal it tight.

Finally, after the damaged module is isolated from the rest of the station, the astronauts have to temporarily increase the airflow from the station's oxygen tanks to bring the station's air pressure back up to normal.

Power Failure

Isolating a leaking module can create new problems even as it solves others. If the isolated module has solar panels, severing the connection to the rest of the station can cause a drop in power to vital equipment, such as the air circulation fans of the life support system. Backup batteries, designed to provide power while the station is in Earth's shadow, can provide emergency power for a time, but if the solar panels' function cannot be restored, the crew may have no choice but to abandon the station.

The station has automatic systems that keep the station oriented so that the panels point at the sun. The systems use spinning stabilizers called gyroscopes to keep the station in the right orientation, or attitude. If the station drifts out of alignment with the sun, adjustments to the station's attitude can be made with thrusters. If the gyroscopes and the thrusters fail to keep the station correctly pointed at the sun, a power failure can result. A vicious cycle then ensues, since the systems that keep the panels pointed toward the sun need power to operate.

This happened after the Progress cargo ship collided with *Mir* in 1997 and the impact sent the station into a slow, uncontrolled tumble that was beyond the ability of the attitude control systems to correct. During the time it took the crew to seal the punctured module off from the rest of the station, the station's solar panels lost their alignment with the sun.

Sometimes, as might be the case if a module with solar panels is isolated, the station suffers a decrease in power rather than a complete power failure. When this happens, station inhabitants must cut power to nonessential systems and reduce heating to the bare minimum until they can fix the problem. Repairs may involve conducting space walks if the problem is damaged solar panels.

Restoring Power

If a space station has suffered a power failure because it is tumbling, as was the case with *Mir* after the 1997 collision, the first step toward restoring power is to arrest the station's tumble so that it can be better controlled; only then will the attitude control systems have a chance to reorient the station toward the sun. To stop the station's tumble, the crew fires the station's thrusters in the direction opposite the tumble.

Even after the tumble is halted, however, the station's automatic systems may not have enough power to reorient the station toward the sun. In this case, the crew may be able to manually move some of the station's solar panels so that they face the sun. The crew of *Mir* was able to stop the station's tumble and then reorient a few, but not all, of the station's solar panels toward the sun. Thus, they were able to restore some power, but not enough to recharge the batteries. This meant that all systems had to be shut down while the station was on the night side of Earth.

If there is not enough power to keep the ventilation system circulating air through the

Mir, We Have a Problem

In one case, it wasn't a spacecraft or onboard system that went awry and presented problems for astronauts aboard a station, but an entire nation. In 1991 the government of the Soviet Union, the country that had built and maintained the space station *Mir*, collapsed. Responsibility for *Mir* was transferred to the country of Russia, but the landing zone for the astronauts then aboard *Mir* was now in the independent nation of Kazakhstan.

For a time it was unclear who had ultimate responsibility for returning the *Mir* astronauts. One astronaut had to stay aboard the station twice as long as originally planned while the problems were worked out, and he returned to Earth a citizen of a different country than when he left!

station, as was the case aboard *Mir*, the astronauts risk asphyxiating in their own expelled breath if they go to sleep. The *Mir* astronauts kept each other awake during the night passes of the station's orbit, fanned each other's faces with maps to restore some air circulation, and moved constantly from module to module; they had to keep moving to stay alive.

Even in the midst of a life-threatening crisis, the astronauts aboard a space station may still be struck in unexpected ways by the awesome beauty of their surroundings. Foale found the station's silence during the power failure inspiring. No longer were the fans and blowers of the ventilation system roaring in the astronauts' ears. Now, for the first time, Foale could look out the window and watch Earth sliding by in utter silence. "Vasily, cheer up," Foale told the station's glum commander, Vasily Tsibliyev: "It's not all bad. Without the problem, we wouldn't be here enjoying this unique experience of beauty and peace."[50]

If the station's systems are not able to fully restore the proper orientation to the sun, the crew can use the systems of the station's attached escape craft. This is the action the crew of *Mir* took to restore power to the station. Tsibliyev, guided by Foale looking out the station's portholes, climbed into the Soyuz escape craft and fired its thrusters to move the station. Bit by bit, under the direction of Foale, who was using the stars for guidance, Tsibliyev used the Soyuz thrusters to nudge the station and its panels to face the sun. With sunlight at last fully on the solar panels, the station's batteries had enough power to begin to recharge. Thirty hours after the collision that caused the power outage, there was enough power for the station's gyroscopes to begin spinning again and for the automatic systems to resume their task of keeping the station's solar panels pointed at the sun.

Medical Emergencies

Along with all the possibility for mechanical failure aboard a space station, astronauts must also face the prospect of medical emergencies. Mission planners try to minimize the risk of medical emergencies by giving astronauts thorough medical screenings before they leave for the station. The purpose of the screening is to catch any potential health problems that might flare up aboard the station. Days before the flight, the astronauts may also be put into medical quarantine to make sure they don't catch any illnesses that could pose a problem on the station.

Even so, given the long stays aboard space stations, inhabitants can become ill, and, of course, injuries are always a possibility. For this reason, as well as to perform medical research, many station crews include a doctor. Station doctors are equipped with medical kits that enable them to administer first aid to their injured crewmates.

After the fire aboard *Mir*, astronaut-doctor Jerry Linenger faced the possibility of treating his crewmates for smoke inhalation. He described how he turned *Mir*'s airlock into a first-aid station:

> I used bungee-cord straps to hold my mini-emergency room instruments—tracheotomy tubes, laryngoscope, ambulatory-breathing bag, oxygen tank, scalpel, stethoscope, and blood oximeter—in place. I then mentally rehearsed what I would do should someone go into respiratory distress, which included such weightlessness-related complications as how to secure the patient to the floor before I would attempt to intubate him or slit his cricothyroid membrane.[51]

Fortunately none of Linenger's crewmates suffered from symptoms related to smoke in-

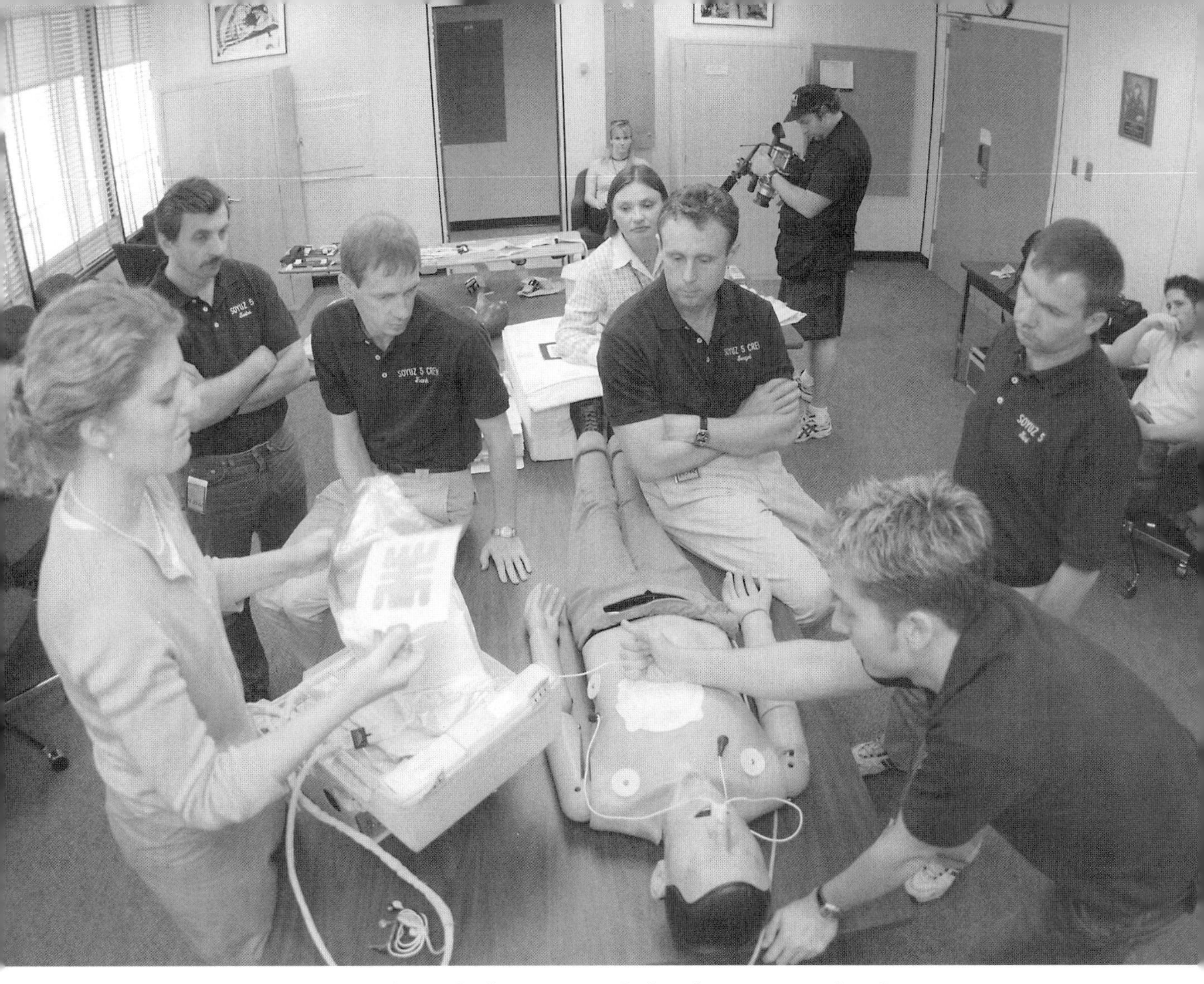

A space station crew trains for medical emergencies before their mission. Though members are screened for good health, illness and injuries can occur on board.

halation, and he did not have to make use of his first-aid station.

When the Doctor Is the Patient

It may sometimes happen that the station's on-board doctor encounters a medical problem he or she cannot handle alone—especially if he or she is the patient! This happened to Norman Thagard, a doctor who lived aboard *Mir* in 1995. One day while Thagard was working out with one of the elastic bands used aboard the station for exercising, the end of the band slipped off his foot and snapped back and hit him in the eye. When he recovered from the immediate pain, Thagard found that his injured eye was hypersensitive to light and that "when I had this eye open, it was like looking at the world through gauze."[52]

If the station's doctor is the patient, he or she has the option to consult with a physician on Earth via videoconference. In Thagard's case, one of his crewmates held a camera to his eye so that an ophthalmologist on Earth could examine it remotely. The ophthalmologist diagnosed the problem and prescribed medicine that was on board the station. Thagard's eye was back to normal within a few days.

Problems Beyond the Station

Sometimes a ground-based or other outside emergency can pose a serious problem for a space station crew. If a problem with a spacecraft scheduled to exchange crew members and deliver supplies delays its launch, station inhabitants may be required to stay aboard the station longer than planned. For this reason, the station is supplied with more oxygen, water, food, and other supplies than are needed between scheduled resupply missions. If the spacecraft is delayed too long, the astronauts will have to return to Earth in the station's escape craft.

The destruction of the space shuttle *Columbia* as it returned from an orbital mission in 2003 forced the astronauts aboard the International Space Station to fall back on emergency procedures. All seven astronauts aboard *Columbia* were killed, and in the wake of the tragedy NASA grounded the remaining three space shuttles indefinitely while it investigated the causes of the disaster. This meant that astronauts Kenneth Bowersox, Nikolai Budarin, and Donald Pettit, who had been scheduled to return from the space station in a shuttle a month later, instead had to return on the station's Soyuz escape ship a month after that.

The Soyuz flight made Bowersox and Pettit the first NASA astronauts (though not the first Americans) to fly the Russian spacecraft back to Earth. The veteran of several shuttle launches and landings, Bowersox was able to compare the experience of riding the two vehicles. He found the Soyuz much less gentle than the shuttle:

> The shuttle landing is a lot like a commercial airliner, whereas the Soyuz is more like landing in a fighter plane aboard an aircraft carrier. It's more aggressive. It's a little more abrupt. It's well within the tolerance capability of the human body. But it's a little more like a carnival ride. You get bounced around and spun around.[53]

Bailing Out

A space station cannot land on Earth; once placed in orbit it is there to stay until its fiery death by reentry into Earth's atmosphere at the end of its life. If a fire cannot be put out, a leak patched, the life support system restarted, or some other emergency overcome, and a station's crew members have to return to Earth in a hurry, they must use an escape ship. For this reason, every space station has an escape craft attached to it at all times. This escape craft is usually a Soyuz capsule, and it is kept ready to leave the station with minimal preparation. Often the escape ship is simply the ship that brought the crew to the station in the first place. During crew changeovers, there may be two Soyuz capsules, or a Soyuz and a space shuttle, docked to the station.

While docked to the station, the escape craft draws power through a cable from the station itself in order to preserve its own internal batteries. It also draws air from the station through a ventilation hose. Both the hose and the cable run through the spacecraft's hatch, and they must be disconnected before the hatch can be sealed and the craft can depart from the station. The cable and hose are designed so that they can be disconnected quickly in an emergency.

Getting Home in a Hurry

A space shuttle can be used to evacuate a station, but since a shuttle is docked to a station for only a few days at a time, it is most likely that only a Soyuz will be available for use as an escape craft. The procedures for evacuating a space station in a Soyuz are the same as those used for a normally scheduled departure. Each Soyuz ship has special seat pads that have been tailored to the individual astronauts who will ride in the ship. Once the ventilation hose and power cable are disconnected, the crew climbs into the ship and closes the hatch. Each crew member, wearing a pressure suit to protect

As a last resort in emergencies, astronauts can escape disaster in a small Soyuz capsule like this one. They also use the Soyuz to return to Earth after the mission.

Escape Vehicles

From the beginning of the history of space stations, Soyuz capsules have been used as escape ships. This often means simply that the ship on which the crew traveled to the station is kept attached to the station and ready for quick use until the end of the crew's mission.

The number of long-term residents who can live on a space station is limited to the number of people who can ride the escape ships docked to the station. Because the Soyuz seats only three people, and normally only one escape ship is docked to the station at a time, the normal crew complement of the International Space Station is limited to three astronauts. NASA has been developing a larger escape craft, called the crew return vehicle, which will be able to seat seven astronauts. This vehicle would enable up to seven astronauts to live aboard the station for extended periods.

against possible decompression of the Soyuz, climbs into his or her assigned seat and straps in. Meanwhile, the pilot, usually the commander of the space station, has been making sure that all of the ship's systems are functioning normally.

Once everyone is strapped in, the pilot undocks from the station and uses gentle nudges from the ship's thrusters to slowly back away. After maneuvering to a safe distance from the station, the pilot orients the spacecraft so that it is traveling backward, with the retro-rockets in its tail pointed in the direction of its travel. At a precisely predefined point in the spacecraft's orbit, the rockets fire, slowing the ship down so that it begins to descend. The timing of the firing of the retro-rockets is critical, since this determines where on Earth the ship will land.

Next, the pilot or the ship's autopilot jettisons, or separates, the ship's orbital and service modules, leaving only the descent module, which contains the astronauts. The other two modules will burn up separately in the atmosphere. However, the descent module will suffer no such fate; it has a heat shield in its base that will protect it from the intense heat of reentry.

When the descent module is low enough, it begins to brush against Earth's atmosphere, which slows it even further, until it plunges into the air. The ship is still moving at a speed of thousands of miles per hour, and air friction creates a fireball that the astronauts inside can see lighting up the air around their spacecraft. Finally the ship reaches an altitude where the air is thick enough for its parachutes to slow it down. The parachutes pop out of the top, and the ship descends to the ground. Even with the parachutes, the descent module is still moving too fast for comfort, so just before impact, braking rockets in the base of the module fire to cushion the landing.

Although much can and does go wrong on a space station—from fires and power failures to medical emergencies and air leaks—quick thinking backed by thorough training allows space station crews to survive and even thrive in the face of almost any crisis. But each crew eventually faces one final challenge of life in space—surviving the long haul.

CHAPTER

6 Surviving the Long Haul

Unlike ordinary spacecraft, space stations are designed to allow people to live in space for months at a time. Being confined in a weightless, potentially dangerous environment for such long periods places unique strains on both the minds and the bodies of station inhabitants. But humans have found ways to adapt to these conditions and are continually engaged in the quest to make long stays in space easier and more comfortable.

Staying Busy

Living aboard a space station for a significant period of time requires an astronaut to make many sacrifices, including giving up a certain amount of freedom, being separated from friends and family, and giving up a lot of privacy. For that reason, astronauts must feel as though their sacrifices serve a purpose. Work goes a long way toward helping them feel that way. And not just any work, as astronaut Shannon Lucid explained:

> I think it's very, very, very important that people have productive work that they're doing. It would be very wrong to send someone up into space with nothing to do. They need to feel like they're productive and that they're doing something worthwhile. So you need to have lots of very interesting scientific-type work for a person to do.[54]

However, the experience of early space station astronauts has shown that being overworked is just as bad as not having enough work to do. Mission planners and ground controllers strive to achieve just the right balance of meaningful work to keep the astronauts occupied and adequate time for them to relax and pursue their own interests, such as reading or keeping in touch with friends and family back home. Preserving this balance is not as important on short-duration flights, such as shuttle missions, so space station astronauts who are used to flying shorter missions find that they have to adjust to a different pace of life. International Space Station astronaut Kenneth Bowersox explained:

> On the shuttle you never really have a weekend. On the space station you have every weekend. On weekends, you get up in the morning, you'll spend three or four hours cleaning, just like you might in your real home. And then in the afternoon, you've got time to do your hobbies, whatever those might be. If you decided you want to do some work on the station, that's okay, or if you want to do something just for fun for yourself you can, or if you want to call your family you can. And then Sunday, the same thing.[55]

Astronaut Phone Home

No one is more isolated than the crew of a space station. Members of a space station

Heavenly Sounds

One of the ways astronauts have found to reduce stress on long stays aboard space stations is playing musical instruments. Many astronauts play instruments when on Earth, and they often bring their instruments with them into space. Playing music not only helps pass the time during off hours and is relaxing to both the players and their listening crewmates, it also lends a homey air to an orbiting outpost, making it seem less like a spacecraft and more like a place to live.

While astronauts have found that their instruments don't sound any different in space, the way they play them does change. For instance, astronaut and flute player Ellen Ochoa found that unless she anchored her feet as she played, the little puffs of air leaving her flute acted as a thruster, propelling her backward.

Ed Lu likewise found that he had to anchor himself to the electric keyboard he brought aboard the International Space Station. If he didn't, the action of hitting the piano keys would cause an equal and opposite reaction that sent him tumbling backward. But with some modification to their playing habits, astronauts have found that they enjoy playing music just as much in space as they do on Earth.

Astronaut Ed Lu had to anchor himself to his keyboard before he could play.

crew have left behind all that is familiar to them, including their friends and family members, and must remain confined in an artificial environment with one another. To combat feelings of isolation, the astronauts remain in daily e-mail contact with friends and family members on Earth. Regularly scheduled video and phone conversations also help crews stay in touch with loved ones back home. But since these types of communication depend on the locations of communications satellites or tracking stations, they are not always the most reliable way to keep in touch.

Astronaut Gerry Carr, who lived on *Skylab* in 1973, described speaking with his family through calls routed through Mission Control over a special phone installed at his house by NASA:

> Once a day, one of us [there were three astronauts on *Skylab*] was allowed anywhere from ten to fifteen minutes of time as we flew over the U.S. to talk to the family on the phone. So each one of us got to speak to our family every three days. That gave us an opportunity to talk with the kids and find out what they were doing and answer their questions and that sort of thing.[56]

Telephone communication between astronauts and the ground has improved since Carr was in space; calls no longer have to be routed through Mission Control. Instead, International Space Station astronauts can call their family's regular home phone when a connection to a communications satellite is available. "You can just go and dial your home phone, on what they call the IP phone,"[57] explained Bowersox.

This phone, which is actually a laptop computer with a headset attached, communicates with a satellite to connect to the Internet. From there, the astronaut's call is routed to the telephone network on Earth. While this is much more convenient than the old way of phoning home from a space station, it still depends on the station having a direct, line-of-sight link to a communications satellite, which is not always available. Also, because of the distances required by the satellite to send the signal to and from the station, up to ninety thousand miles, there may be a noticeable time delay that inhibits spontaneous conversation.

Other Ways to Stay in Touch

One of the most consistent and reliable means of keeping in touch with family members at home is through e-mail. The station's residents can send and receive e-mails daily, allowing them to keep up with the day-to-day activities of their family members. This is a very important factor in preventing astronauts from feeling isolated.

Amateur radio operators also provide a vital link to the home planet for the astronauts on a space station. Ham radio operators all over the world can communicate with the space station as it passes overhead, and for as long as it remains within the line of sight of the operator's radio antenna. Because the station moves so fast, flying from one coast of the United States to the other in just a few minutes, the ham radio conversations are very brief. Nevertheless, ham radio remains an important way for space station residents to combat feelings of isolation.

Holidays in Space

Astronauts aboard space stations mark the passage of time in their unique environment in

ISS crewmembers display their onboard Christmas tree. Holiday celebrations help the crew relax and maintain a sense of normalcy.

part by celebrating holidays. For instance, at Christmastime, family and friends might send gifts such as Christmas stockings to them on a cargo ship. Astronauts might also put up a paper Christmas tree. Just as they do on Earth, space station astronauts take time off from work on holidays and talk with distant family members by phone. They also celebrate holidays with special meals, such as canned chicken or smoked turkey from a sealed package that does not require refrigeration.

Time Out for Fun

Making time to have fun is essential to the well-being of long-term space station inhabitants. Pastimes for astronauts include Earth-gazing from the station's windows, executing acrobatic maneuvers possible only in space, and even using the propulsive force of a vacuum cleaner to fly around the station. Crew members may also bring aboard a limited number of personal items to help them cope with living in a metal shell with only a few other people to look at day after day. Books, DVD and audio players, and photos of family members all help in this regard. Additional items can also be sent by request aboard resupply ships.

Lucid spent much of her free time aboard the Russian space station *Mir* reading books. She found enough time to read one or two books a week, and she kept her library in a makeshift bookshelf, which, as she explained, her crewmates found odd:

The Russian food comes up in metal cans, and so I took some of those and with a strap and bungee cords, I put it up on one wall, and then I put my books in it. It was like a bookshelf. Yuri Onufriendko came in and he said, "What's this?" and I said, "It's my bookshelf," and I could just see him roll his eyes and think, Well, whatever makes the American happy. So I always had my books out. It just makes you feel good to see your books.[58]

On one occasion, however, Lucid found that her library made her feel *more* isolated instead of less so. When she finished a science fiction book she had been reading, she discovered that it ended in a cliffhanger; it turned out to be the first part of a series. She didn't have the second book with her on the station.

That was the point where you realized you were just really isolated, because obviously, if I'd been living here [on Earth], I would have gone out immediately to the bookstore and gotten the second volume. But I sent a lot of e-mail messages with a lot of threats. I told [my daughter] that it better be on the next Progress. So they worked really hard and they got it on the next Progress.[59]

The Greatest Show on Earth

Space station astronauts never tire of watching Earth slide past the station's windows, and have said that it is the single greatest pastime aboard the station. *Mir* astronaut John Blaha

An astronaut photographs Earth's surface features from the ISS. "Earth-watching" is a favorite crew pastime.

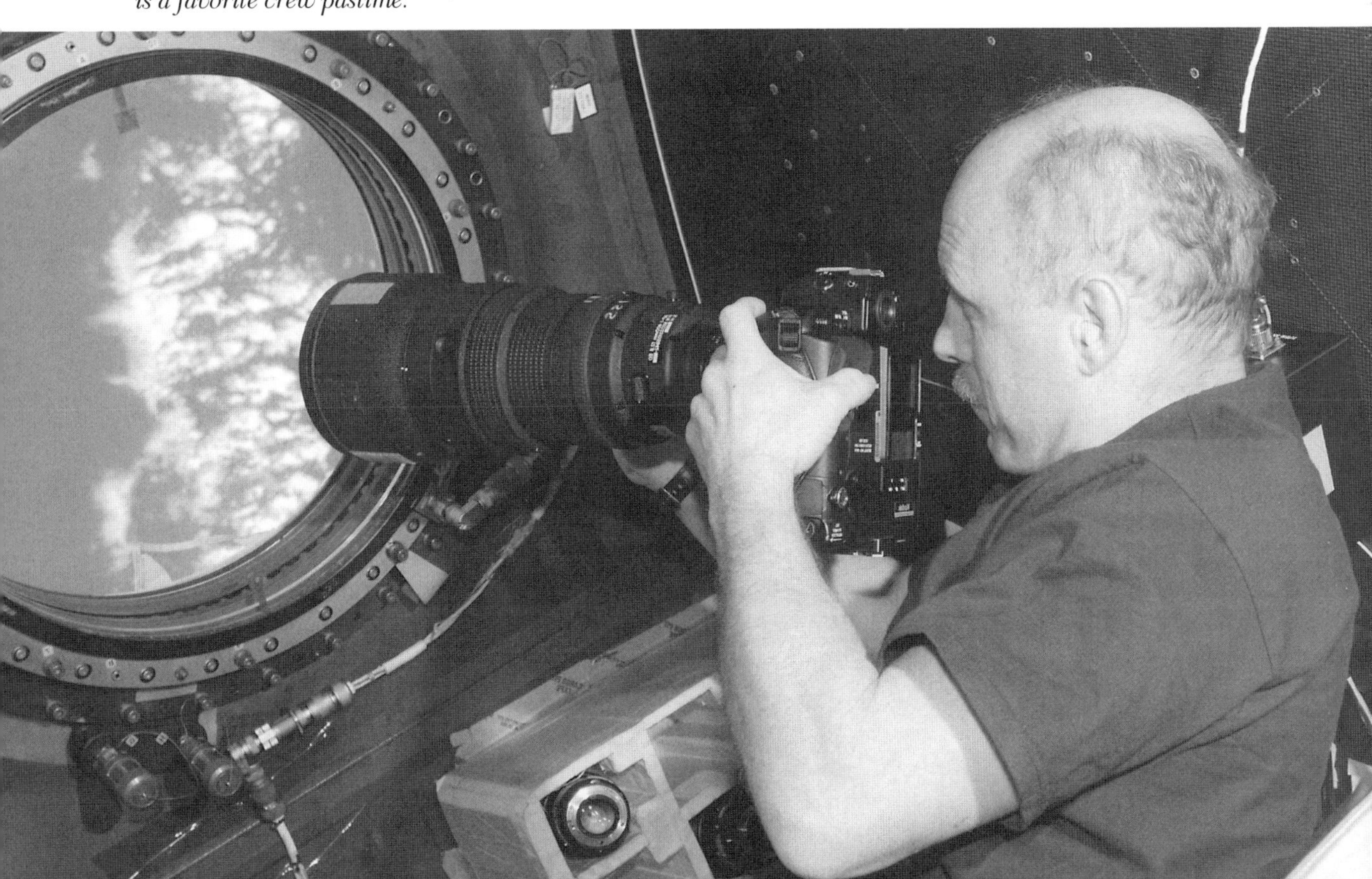

described how he kept track of what surface features the station would pass over at what times, and then take a break from work in order to watch his favorite sites.

> I enjoyed using a ground track map that NASA had loaded on one of our computers. This map would allow you to see ahead what your ground track would be for the day, and note the times you would pass over the locations. I used to note the times and places I wanted to view on my daily plan so that I could take a break from work to view planet Earth and see some specific locations. . . . I knew . . . that if I planned viewing opportunities, I could accomplish my work and have time to view the planet.[60]

It is not just more convenient for the astronauts to schedule their Earth-watching times, it is a necessity. Since more than 70 percent of Earth's surface is water, more often than not the astronauts see only the unbroken blue of the oceans and the white swirls of cloud cover when they look out the window.

Staying in Shape

In addition to the emotional strain of living for an extended period in a confined, artificial environment, life in space places stress on the human body. In fact, much of the scientific research conducted aboard space stations concerns the effects of long-duration space travel on the human body. It is important to understand these effects in detail if astronauts are to one day travel to Mars—a journey of about six months each way—and still be able to function on the planet's surface when they get there.

One of the biggest problems with weightlessness is that it causes muscles to atrophy and bones to lose mass. Astronauts aboard a space station can counteract many of these effects through a regular exercise routine. They must exercise one to two hours a day to keep fit enough to return to Earth in good health. Exercising in a weightless environment presents some special challenges, however. Astronauts cannot get exercise by lifting weights or doing push-ups or pull-ups, as they can on Earth. Instead, they must rely on exercise equipment that uses resistance, rather than weight, to give them a workout.

Celestial Gym

One of the pieces of space exercise equipment used on board a space station is a special treadmill. The astronauts use the treadmill several times a week to keep them in good enough shape to be able to walk and stand properly when they return to Earth. Since the astronauts using the treadmill do not stick to the treadmill's surface, they must hold themselves down with bungee cords attached to a harness they wear while they work out. This solution to the problem of getting a workout in space is not perfect; the harness, being pulled down by the bungee cords, often digs painfully into the astronauts' shoulders and hips, chafing as the astronauts move their legs.

But the bungee cords do a very good job of holding the astronauts down to the treadmill—so good that the astronauts must wear shoes or slippers while using the machine to avoid hurting their feet, especially since their feet become abnormally sensitive after several weeks in space. In fact, the astronauts' feet become ever more sensitive as their stay in space lengthens. "At the beginning of most of my runs, the soles of my feet feel as if they were being stabbed with pins and needles—so un-

A crewmember reads while exercising on a cycling device. Zero gravity weakens muscles so daily exercise is important.

accustomed are they to pressure of any kind,"[61] said Linenger. Also, without the constant pressure of standing and walking under gravity, calluses on the feet gradually diminish, finally flaking off entirely by the fourth month in space and increasing the sensitivity of the astronauts' feet even further.

Space station treadmills can also pose unexpected difficulties for the station residents who are *not* using them. Astronauts using treadmills on space stations have found that if they walk or run at a particular speed, they might set up a resonance in the structure of the station that can be felt throughout the station. If the resonance is too great, it can actually cause problems for delicate scientific experiments. It is partly for this reason that some experiments are contained in floating racks that isolate them from vibrations

The Phantom Torso

NASA has had a strange helper in the effort to better understand the effects of cosmic radiation on the human body. The Phantom Torso, affectionately known as "Fred," is a full-sized mock-up of a human body, minus the arms and legs. Weighing about ninety-five pounds and standing three feet tall, "Fred" is constructed of materials designed to mimic human internal organs, flesh, and even the human skeletal system. He is also laden with radiation sensors, called dosimeters—about sixteen hundred of them buried deep within his body.

First sent to the International Space Station in 2001, Fred "lived" for four months in a quiet corner of the station, silently absorbing radiation from space, just as his more active crewmates did. The crucial difference, however, was that Fred's dosimeters could be examined to determine just how much radiation had penetrated what organs. By comparing readings from Fred's dosimeters to those attached to the outside of the space station, scientists could determine how much radiation had been stopped by the walls of the station and if the radiation had changed during its passage through the station. All of this gives NASA scientists and engineers more data in their quest to enable astronauts to live aboard space stations and other spacecraft for ever longer periods of time.

"Fred" the phantom torso silently absorbs cosmic radiation inside the ISS. Fred's hundreds of dosimeters measure radiation levels onboard.

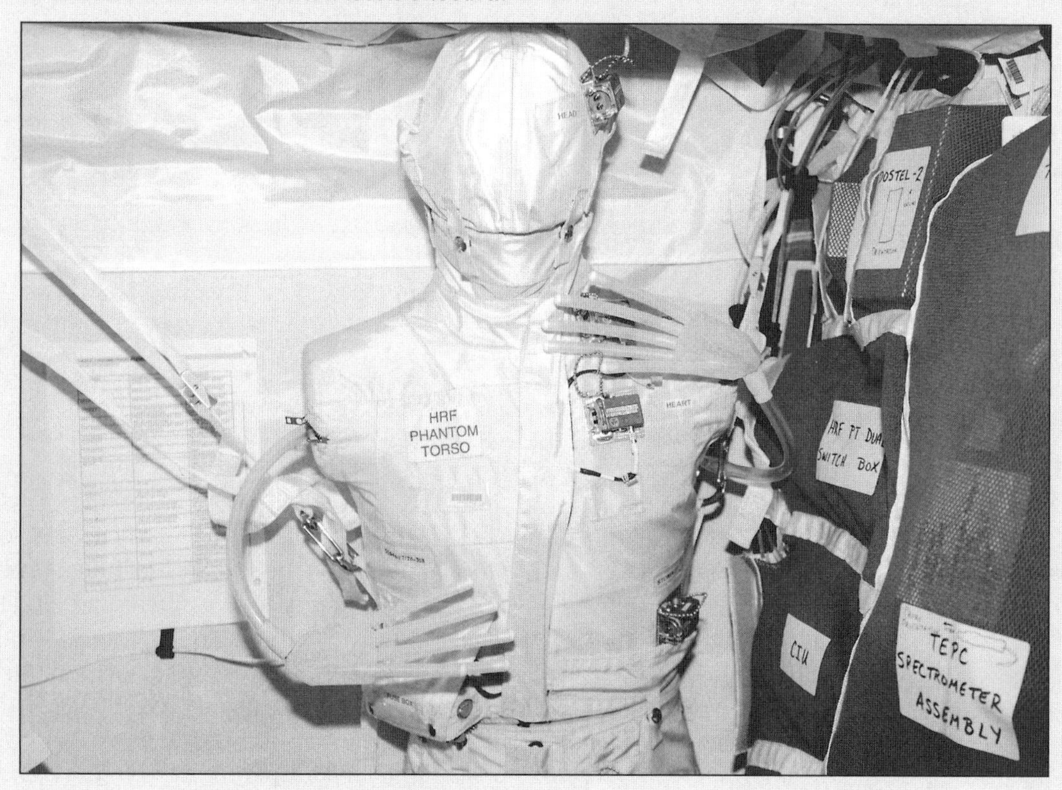

and small accelerations. Linenger described a resonance caused by one of his crewmates working out in *Mir:*

> It feels similar to being in a rowboat, near the shore, after a ski boat has gone past. A gentle, but definite swaying of the entire thirteen-meter tube in which I am presently located. The station is absorbing the force that Sasha imparts to the treadmill, and *Mir* sways, resonates. If he were to either slow down or speed up a bit, I would feel nothing.[62]

Seeing RED

Another piece of exercise equipment used on space stations is called a resistive exercise device, or RED. It uses a bungee cord system similar to that used with the treadmill to hold astronauts in a standing position against a space station wall. The amount of pressure, or resistance, holding the astronaut to the wall can be adjusted to produce workouts of varying intensity.

Astronauts exercise with the RED much as they would with weights on Earth—by squatting up and down to produce an effect similar to that of a weightlifter doing knee bends with barbells on his or her shoulders, by doing bicep curls, by pushing upward with their arms as though doing bench presses, and so on. The RED can simulate the effect of holding oneself up against the pull of gravity, helping the astronauts to stay conditioned for their eventual return to Earth.

Working out in space differs from a normal workout in ways other than just the type of equipment used. In the absence of convection, the process by which heated air rises on Earth, carbon dioxide collects around an exercising astronaut's face faster than the air circulation system can blow it away. As a result, some astronauts find that they become short of breath more quickly than they would during a similar amount of exercise on Earth. This effect can be counteracted to some extent by exhaling forcefully at regular intervals during the workout to increase the circulation of air.

Sweat, too, behaves differently in space than it does on Earth. Instead of dripping off the body as it would in an earthly gym, it tends to pool unpleasantly, quivering on the astronauts' body like masses of gelatin until it is wiped away. All these factors add up to what at least one astronaut has described as an aggravating experience, making workouts much less enjoyable than they are on Earth.

Radiation Hazard

In addition to the negative health effects of prolonged periods of weightlessness, space station crews have another serious problem to worry about. Earth's atmosphere shields the surface from much harmful solar and cosmic radiation. In orbit outside of Earth's atmosphere, space station crews are exposed to significantly more radiation than are people on the ground. The effects of this higher radiation exposure are not well understood, but they are thought to include a significantly increased risk of developing cancer and an increased risk of birth defects and other reproductive problems.

For this reason, the space agencies that send astronauts to a space station carefully monitor the time each astronaut spends in space and the radiation levels to which he or she may have been exposed. These measurements are helped by individual dosimeters worn by crew members and by radiation-monitoring devices placed throughout the station. The amount of radiation exposure deemed acceptable for each

Seeing Stars

Increased exposure to radiation is not just an abstract concept to space station inhabitants; they can actually see cosmic radiation in the form of flashes behind their closed eyes. While not completely understood, these flashes are thought to be the result of cosmic rays passing through the optic nerve and stimulating it to register light, even when there is none present.

In his book *Diary of a Cosmonaut,* Valentin Lebedev described the great variety among the eerie flashes of light he saw aboard the *Salyut-7* space station. "Some of them are like lightning or exploding balls," he said, "others like short strokes."

astronaut varies according to the astronaut's age, gender, amount of time spent in space on previous missions, and other, external, factors. For instance, younger women are thought to be at greater risk for developing cancer from radiation exposure than are older men. Also, astronauts who are aboard a space station during periods of peak solar activity receive higher doses of radiation than crew members who are aboard during the sun's more quiet periods. Since the walls of the station provide some protection from radiation, astronauts onboard space stations may put off scheduled space walks during solar flares and other times of increased solar activity.

The space agencies that send astronauts to a space station use all of these factors to calculate an individual lifetime limit on time spent in space for each astronaut. According to the complex formulas used by NASA, a forty-five-year-old astronaut should spend no more than a lifetime total of about 250 days in space.

Because of the relative scarcity of knowledge about space radiation, this estimate is necessarily rough and errs on the side of caution. Much of the scientific research conducted aboard the International Space Station is concerned with the study of radiation in space and its effects on the human body, in the hope that the risks of radiation exposure to astronauts can be better defined.

Long-term space travel carries unique risks. Part of the job of space station residents is to add to the body of knowledge about the precise nature of these risks and how to mitigate them. The hardship the astronauts endure contributes to better conditions for those who follow—and makes the return home all the sweeter.

CHAPTER 7

Returning to Earth

After weeks or months in Earth orbit, it is finally time for the space station inhabitants to make their way home. Scientific equipment and other gear must be packed up and either stowed on the station for the next crew or brought aboard the spacecraft that will take the astronauts home. The astronauts also review the procedures they will use to get home since it has been a long time since they trained for this mission. If the station will not be inhabited for a while after they leave, the astronauts shut down the station's major systems and prepare it for the absence of a crew.

In most cases the next space station crew comes aboard before the previous crew departs. In these cases a spacecraft comes from Earth carrying the new station crew—and the departing astronauts' ride home. Watching the arrival of the spacecraft that will take them home is a heartwarming sight for the returning astronauts. "When I saw *Atlantis* approaching the *Mir*," said Linenger, "I felt pure elation, pure unbridled joy."[63]

Packing Up

The departing astronauts do not have much time to think about their homecoming, however. They have a lot of work to do. Whether they will be on board to greet the next crew or not, they have to pack up their belongings. They have space to take home just a few personal items; the rest they stow in soft-sided containers, which they label for easy access by the crew that will follow them. Items placed in these containers include uneaten sweets, which are always prized by station astronauts, and other food items allocated to the departing crew. Unused personal items such as tooth brushes are also stowed.

In addition to packing and stowing personal items, the astronauts finish up scientific experiments. If they have fallen behind in any of their work, they may scramble to finish it before they have to leave. When they have finished using the scientific equipment, they shut it down, clean it, perform routine maintenance on it, and otherwise ready it for use by the next crew. For example, they might top off the water tanks on plant growth experiments. If some of the experiments the astronauts have been running will not be used immediately by the next crew, the departing astronauts disassemble the equipment and stow it out of the way.

The departing astronauts also have to check the pressurized reentry suits they will wear on the return journey, making sure they are functioning properly and are in good repair. Finally, since it may have been many months since the astronauts trained to operate their spacecraft for the return trip, they have to review the spacecraft's systems and the procedures they will need to follow to operate them. This review process typically begins about a week before the astronauts' departure from the station. Along with all their other chores, the astronauts manage to find time to exercise more vigorously in the days before

Before departure, exiting ISS crews pack up their belongings in soft-sided containers like these. They can take only a few items home with them.

their return to prepare their bodies for the strain of living under gravity again.

During the changeover period, which can last anywhere from ten to twenty days, the departing crew helps the new crew transfer supplies from the spacecraft and briefs the new crew on all they need to know about the station's quirks and idiosyncrasies. At the end of the changeover period, the departing astronauts say goodbye to their colleagues remaining on the station and climb into their spacecraft for the return to Earth. They close the hatch and use the spacecraft's thrusters to push off from the station.

Into the Wild Black Yonder

After the spacecraft undocks, it may fly around the station so the astronauts on board can conduct a visual survey of the station. They report what they see to the astronauts still on board the station, noting anything unusual. They also take pictures and video that they can send to ground-based engineers and controllers. Once this maneuver is completed, they fire the ship's rockets to pull farther away from the station.

As the spacecraft pulls away from the station, the departing astronauts see the station dwindling in their windows, until it is lost to the blackness of space. Linenger described his departure from *Mir* aboard the space shuttle *Atlantis:*

> Following a gentle push-off, we began intermittently firing our thrusters. The bursts made loud bang-bang-bang sounds, similar in abruptness to cannon firing. As we moved away, the *Mir* became smaller, then smaller still. Finally, it was so diminished in size that the space station appeared to be nothing more than a rather insignificant blinking light among the stars.[64]

The dwindling space station is a bittersweet sight to the astronauts, who are leaving behind their home of the last several months, and do not know when, if ever, they will return.

Homeward Bound

The returning ship is still following the same orbit around Earth as the station, and so the astronauts must fire retro-rockets to slow their speed just enough to lower their altitude and begin to graze Earth's atmosphere. The rockets are in the tail of the ship, so the ship must be oriented so that it is traveling backward when the rockets fire. Atmospheric friction does the rest of the work of pulling the craft out of orbit.

Reentry into Earth's atmosphere is violent, the most dangerous part of space travel except for launch. The friction caused by the spacecraft falling through the atmosphere at thousands of miles per hour creates a tremendous amount of heat. The bottom of the ship is heavily insulated with a heat shield, designed to

A homebound astronaut watches the ISS recede in the distance. Though eager to go home, astronauts cherish their experiences aboard the station.

withstand the heat of reentry, more than 3,000°F. The rest of the ship, while also insulated, is not designed to withstand the full heat of reentry, so it is vital that the ship enter the atmosphere at the correct angle.

If the ship comes in at the wrong angle, or if there is a breach in the heat shield, the superheated gas that forms around the ship as it reenters can melt the structure of the ship itself. If that happens, the ship will disintegrate, as happened to the space shuttle *Columbia* as it reentered Earth's atmosphere in February 2003.

Reentry

As the ship slices into the atmosphere, the astronauts aboard see a glow begin to form around it. The air thickens as the craft descends, and the air around the ship glows hotter and hotter. Soon the outer skin of the ship glows red hot. The ship enters the atmosphere at such a high speed and the friction created between the ship's hull and the surrounding air is so great that the very atoms of the atmospheric gases are stripped of their electrons, creating a mass of charged particles called plasma. The plasma creates a physical barrier that prevents radio signals from entering or leaving the ship, cutting the astronauts off from ground controllers for part of the return trip. If there have been any problems with the reentry sequence, this can be a tense part of the return journey as ground controllers anxiously await the moment when radio contact is restored and the astronauts can report their successful reentry.

The trip can be very bumpy, and decelerating from orbital speed creates an uncomfortable buildup of g forces. This is especially uncomfortable for the astronauts who have been in a weightless environment for several months, unused to Earth's normal 1-g pull. Bowersox and his crewmates experienced an even rougher Soyuz entry than normal as they returned from the International Space Station. He explained:

> Our system downmoded to a ballistic entry. It happened automatically when one of the control systems didn't work exactly as you would hope. . . . What that meant to us was that our g load on entry was a little bit higher [than expected]. On a controlled entry you'll come in at about a peak weight of 3 or 4 times your body weight, and on a ballistic entry, you'll get up to 8 or 9 times your body weight on the deceleration.[65]

Touchdown

If the astronauts are returning in a Soyuz capsule, parachutes deploy as soon as the craft reaches a low enough altitude. The ship comes down in the grasslands of Kazakhstan, briefly firing braking rockets an instant before touching down to soften the landing. Astronauts returning in a space shuttle land on a runway as they would in a conventional airplane, either at Cape Canaveral in Florida or at Edwards Air Force Base in California. The space shuttle, too, has parachutes, which deploy from the rear of the craft after touchdown to help bring the craft to a stop on the runway.

Opening the hatch, the astronauts inhale the smells of Earth for the first time in months. The smell of dirt, grass, and fresh air all greet the astronauts, who have been breathing canned air for so long they have almost forgotten what Earth smells like.

The spacecraft is met by a recovery team after it touches down, and the astronauts, weak

Heat Shields and Ceramic Tiles

Both the space shuttles and the Soyuz capsules that return astronauts to Earth from the International Space Station rely on heat shielding to protect the astronauts from the extremely high temperatures created by reentry.

Each Soyuz capsule has what is known as an ablative heat shield on its base. As the material of the outer layers of the heat shield grows hotter, it vaporizes, dissipating the tremendous heat of reentry that would otherwise destroy the entire capsule. The shield covers only the base of the Soyuz, so the capsule must reenter with its base pointed downward. Because the heat shield is destroyed during reentry, it can be used only once. In fact, the entire Soyuz capsule is used only once.

Space shuttles use different materials to shield the astronauts from the heat of reentry. The shuttle is covered with thousands of ceramic tiles, collectively called the thermal protection system, that can withstand the heat without being destroyed, making them, like the shuttle itself, reusable. However, the tiles are fragile in other ways and require a great deal of maintenance between flights. It was because of damage to some of these ceramic tiles on liftoff that the shuttle *Columbia* burned up on reentry in 2003.

Astronauts check the heat shielding on the belly of their craft for any problems. Shielding damage caused the 2003 Columbia *disaster.*

A returning Soyuz capsule, parachute deployed, sends up a dust cloud as it touches down in Kazakhstan.

and wobbly after being weightless for so long, are helped out of their spacecraft and attended to by doctors. Soyuz astronauts are hauled out of the hatch at the top of their space capsule and gently handed down to more helpers on the ground. They are then carried to folding chairs, where they can sit without moving, slowly getting used to the feeling of their own weight again.

Coming Home Alone

The astronauts are *usually* met by a recovery team—but not always. Since the Soyuz lacks wings or other means of controlling its flight path once it enters the atmosphere, it does not always land precisely on target. However, since it does not require a runway, it does not have to land with the precision of the space shuttle, and a very large, uninhabited area of Kazakhstan is chosen as the landing zone for this reason.

If a Soyuz crew lands a great distance off-target, the recovery team must spend some time searching for them. This is what happened to Bowersox and his crewmates after their unscheduled return from the ISS aboard a Soyuz. Although their ship came down as expected in the grasslands of Kazakhstan, they came up far short of the planned landing point. It took the recovery team four or five hours to reach them.

This did not bother Bowersox and his crewmates, however. Instead, said Bowersox, "Don [Pettit] and Nikolai [Budarin] and I thought that that would be a lot like what it would be for the first guys to get to Mars; they'll show up and there won't be anybody there to meet them. It'll be quiet and peaceful."[66] Bowersox and his crewmates climbed out of their spacecraft, removed their reentry suits, and set up radio beacons to aid the recovery team in their search. They also had a chance to start to regain their "Earth legs."

Earth Legs

Astronauts returning from space stations have likened the process of readjusting to life under gravity to that of sea voyagers getting used to no longer being on the deck of a rolling ship. It takes time for their bodies to adjust, particularly their vestibular systems, the organs of the inner ear that control balance. Just as the inner ear has to adapt to the absence of gravity, it has to readjust after the return to Earth. Bowersox described how he felt just after returning to Earth:

> We had a lot of good exercise equipment on board the space station and all of us had used it a lot, so one of the first things I did was try to stand up and see how it would feel, and it was okay. But what I found was my vestibular organs were very sensitive, and so every time I would move my head around, that was uncomfortable, and I would get symptoms of motion sickness. So if I moved my head less, I would feel better, and the best way to do that was just to not really stand up but to kind of crawl around. But we could walk if we wanted to.[67]

Until their vestibular systems adjust, the returning astronauts may find themselves dizzy and nauseated after their arrival on Earth. Staying balanced on their feet requires

Medical teams check out three astronauts (seated) just returned from space. Newly returned astronauts often have trouble standing at first.

concentration, and if they close their eyes while standing, they may find themselves falling over. The vestibular effects of living in space gradually diminish over a period of a couple of days.

Toughening Up

While the astronauts are regaining their Earth legs, they must also cope with muscles that have weakened from underuse. Even with all the exercise they have been doing aboard the station to stay fit, they still emerge from their ship much weaker than when they departed. Because of this, astronauts may find it difficult to sleep their first night back on Earth, as returning *Salyut-7* astronaut Valentin Lebedev discovered.

> An unbelievable force crushed my body into the bed. I would have sworn the Earth's gravity had increased while I was away. I tried to lift my hand, but it was like trying to lift a three-pound weight. Just rolling over took a tremendous effort, as if I were in a centrifuge under a 2-g load. I felt like a baby waving my hands and legs in the air reaching for support to roll over onto my side.[68]

Some astronauts find that after their return from a space station they have some difficulty walking or just standing properly, as Bowersox explained:

> I was used to walking at exactly five and a half miles per hour, and if I ran faster than five and a half miles per hour or slower than five and a half miles per hour on the ground, I would get really tired, but if I ran at five and a half miles per hour like I did on the treadmill, I could go forever because that was what my body was used to. Your posture muscles take a little bit longer to come around. You don't appreciate how much work your muscles are doing to keep your spine erect and your neck up all day. So it takes a few months . . . you find yourself getting sore just sitting in a meeting.[69]

Returning *Skylab* astronaut Gerry Carr found that his joints in particular suffered from disuse, as he explained:

> It took a little while for our joints to begin to toughen up again. Walking for a long period of time or running or anything like that could get painful in the knees and ankles and hips. But in about three or four days, those joints toughened up again and we were just fine.[70]

Home Sweet Home

Back home, the astronauts have many other adjustments to make beyond the physical ones. They have been away from their normal lives for months, and, as in the case of astronauts who trained away from their home countries, may have been away from their homes for a year or more before that.

The return to earthbound routines can happen quickly, as it did for returning *Mir* astronaut Shannon Lucid:

> We landed on a Thursday and came back to Houston on Friday and by Friday morning, I could feel everything click into place. I knew my vestibular system was back to normal. I got home, back to Houston, Friday evening, and Saturday I went to the grocery store, had to get some groceries, and went

Landing a Spacecraft

The Soyuz and the space shuttle are two very different spacecraft, and this is reflected in the way each one comes in for a landing.

Because the space shuttle has wings, it has control surfaces that allow its pilot to steer it very precisely to its landing. The landing must be precise because the shuttle needs a very long runway to bleed off its remaining speed at touchdown. One of two runways is normally used for the shuttle—one near its launch point in Florida, and the other in California.

After the shuttle enters the atmosphere, the pilot executes a series of banking turns to control the spacecraft's rate of descent and its eventual landing point. The steeper the bank, the faster the shuttle's descent. The pilot must be careful not to lose too much speed too quickly; the shuttle's descent is unpowered, meaning that it is simply a heavy glider at this stage of its flight, and it can land short of the runway if it slows down too quickly.

By contrast, the Soyuz has no wings and no control surfaces. Like the shuttle, it does have maneuvering thrusters that the pilot can use to properly orient the spacecraft as it enters the atmosphere, but as the atmosphere thickens around the spacecraft, these thrusters become ineffective. From this point on, the pilot and passengers of the Soyuz are simply along for the ride, landing wherever the wind blows their parachutes. For this reason a large, sparsely populated area of Kazakhstan is allocated to Soyuz landings, and it is up to the recovery teams to locate the precise landing point after the fact.

The space shuttle Atlantis *lands at the Kennedy Space Center on its return from space. Unlike the Soyuz, a shuttle's landing can be guided.*

As they return to Earth after their missions, astronauts know that they have been forever changed by life on a space station.

> to the bookstore, and then Sunday went to church, and Monday came in to work.[71]

Although the return to routines can be quick, the adjustments required for an astronaut to fit back into a previous life take longer, as Lucid found:

> It was very strange to go back to the office because I had been in Russia for a year training before the flight and it was really hard to be back accepted as part of the office, because life goes on without you, and things change. To find your place back again at work was hard.[72]

A Lasting Impact

Even after the other effects of living aboard a space station have worn off, astronauts find themselves reminded in unexpected ways of their extraordinary life high above Earth. Long after his return from the International Space Station, Bowersox noticed lingering changes in the way he interacted with the world around him.

> I do find that my touch is a lot lighter now. In orbit, you develop a gentler touch because if you grab things too heavily, you can bump them and knock them away, so you get used to just reaching out just very gently and grabbing onto things, and I've noticed every once in a while that I won't hold things tightly enough and they'll slip out of my hand.[73]

Besides the lasting physical effects, the returned astronauts find their perspective on life and the world around them forever altered. "I believe that I am a changed person because of my experience in space,"[74] said Linenger after his return. The biggest change he found within himself was a deep understanding of the interconnected nature of all things on Earth. Because of his greatly broadened perspective, he realized that conflict, no matter how large or small, is pointless. "We are all in it together on planet Earth," he said. "We are not separate. There are no true divisions between us, only those we artificially impose."[75]

Although it may take months for the astronauts to get their lives back to normal, they find that they have returned to Earth very much richer in experience than when they left; their lives have been forever changed for the better, and few regret having made the journey.

Notes

Chapter 1: Leaving the Planet

1. Jerry M. Linenger, *Off the Planet: Surviving Five Perilous Months Aboard the Space Station* Mir. New York: McGraw-Hill, 2000, pp. 17–18.
2. Linenger, *Off the Planet,* p. 28.
3. Kenneth Chang, "Riding the Vomit Comet," ABCNews.com, March 26, 1999. http://abcnews.go.com/sections/science/DailyNews/vomitcomet990326_flight.html.
4. Keith Cowing, "Earth's First Self-Financed Astronaut," SpaceRef.com, December 10, 2000. www.spaceref.com/news/viewnews.html?id=263.
5. Ed Lu, "The Soyuz Ride," NASA Human Spaceflight Web site. http://spaceflight.nasa.gov/station/crew/exp7/luletters/lu_letter1.html.
6. Linenger, *Off the Planet,* p. 65.
7. Quoted in Kevin W. Kelley, ed., *The Home Planet.* Reading, MA: Addison-Wesley, 1988, p. 12.
8. Quoted in Kelley, *The Home Planet,* p. 7.
9. Quoted in Kelley, *The Home Planet,* p.92.
10. Quoted in Kelley, *The Home Planet,* p. 28.
11. Quoted in Kelley, *The Home Planet,* p. 109.

Chapter 2: Arriving

12. Linenger, *Off the Planet,* p. 78.
13. Linenger, *Off the Planet,* p. 78.
14. Gerry Carr, telephone interview with the author, November 4, 2003.
15. Norman E. Thagard, "Norman E. Thagard," NASA Oral History, ISS Phase I History Project, 1998. http://spaceflight.nasa.gov/history/shuttle-mir/people/p-r-thagard.htm.
16. Linenger, *Off the Planet,* p. 83.
17. Carr, interview.
18. Quoted in Colin Foale, *Waystation to the Stars: The Story of Mir, Michael and Me.* London: Headline, 1999, p. 71.
19. Quoted in Robert Zimmerman, *Leaving Earth: Space Stations, Rival Superpowers, and the Quest for Interplanetary Travel.* Washington, DC: Joseph Henry Press, 2003, p. 63.
20. Quoted in Foale, *Waystation to the Stars,* p. 71.
21. Linenger, *Off the Planet,* p. 87.

Chapter 3: Living in Space

22. Carr, interview.
23. Shannon Lucid, telephone interview with the author, November 10, 2003.
24. Jerry M. Linenger, *Letters from Mir: An Astronaut's Letter to His Son.* New York: McGraw-Hill, 2003, p. 57.
25. Linenger, *Letters from Mir,* p. 58.
26. *Mission to Mir,* directed by Ivan Gallin. 1997, Burbank, CA: Warner Home Video, 2001.
27. Quoted in Foale, *Waystation to the Stars,* p. 76.
28. Carr, interview.
29. Linenger, *Letters from Mir,* pp. 42–43.
30. Linenger, *Letters from Mir,* p. 106.
31. *Mission to Mir.*
32. Valentin Lebedev, *Diary of a Cosmonaut: 211 Days in Space,* trans. Luba Diangar, eds. Daniel Puckett and C.W. Harrison. New York: Bantam Books, 1988, pp. 49–50.
33. Carr, interview.
34. Linenger, *Letters from Mir,* p. 3.
35. Linenger, *Letters from Mir,* p. 11.
36. Linenger, *Letters from Mir,* pp. 98–99.
37. Lebedev, *Diary of a Cosmonaut,* p. 112.

Chapter Four: Working in Space

38. Lebedev, *Diary of a Cosmonaut,* p. 134.
39. Carr, interview.
40. Lucid, interview.
41. Lebedev, *Diary of a Cosmonaut,* p. 150.
42. Kenneth Bowersox, telephone interview with the author, November 3, 2003.
43. Bowersox, interview.
44. Carr, interview.
45. Lucid, interview.

Chapter Five: Handling Emergencies

46. *Terror in Space,* NOVA. Boston: WGBH-TV, 1998.
47. *Terror in Space.*
48. *Terror in Space.*
49. *Terror in Space.*
50. Quoted in Foale, *Waystation to the Stars,* p. 121.
51. Linenger, *Off the Planet,* p. 108.
52. Thagard, "Norman E. Thagard."
53. Bowersox, interview.

Chapter Six: Surviving the Long Haul

54. Shannon W. Lucid, "Shannon W. Lucid," NASA Oral History, ISS Phase I History Project, 1998. http://spaceflight.nasa.gov/history/shuttle-mir/people/p-r-lucid.htm.
55. Bowersox, interview.
56. Carr, interview.
57. Bowersox interview.
58. Lucid, interview.
59. Lucid, "Shannon W. Lucid."
60. John E. Blaha, "John E. Blaha," NASA Oral History, ISS Phase 1 History Project, 1998. http://spaceflight.nasa.gov/history/shuttle-mir/people/p-r-blaha.htm.
61. Linenger, *Letters from Mir,* p. 61.
62. Linenger, *Letters from Mir,* p. 40.

Chapter Seven: Returning to Earth

63. Linenger, *Letters from Mir,* p. 202.
64. Linenger, *Letters from Mir,* p. 202.
65. Bowersox, interview.
66. Bowersox, interview.
67. Bowersox, interview.
68. Lebedev, *Diary of a Cosmonaut,* p. 271.
69. Bowersox, interview.
70. Carr, interview.
71. Lucid, interview.
72. Lucid, interview.
73. Bowersox, interview.
74. Linenger, *Letters from Mir,* p. 119.
75. Linenger, *Letters from Mir,* p. 120.

For Further Reading

Books

Colin Foale, *Waystation to the Stars: The Story of* Mir, *Michael and Me.* London: Headline, 1999. The father of *Mir* astronaut Michael Foale recounts the adventures of his son aboard the Russian space station. The book also chronicles astronaut Foale's childhood and early influences.

Roger D. Launius, *Space Stations: Base Camps to the Stars.* Washington, DC: Smithsonian Books, 2003. Lavishly illustrated with paintings, drawings, and photographs, this book presents a history of space stations, both real and imagined, and shows how the dreams of science fiction writers and scientists have led to the International Space Station.

Jerry M. Linenger, *Letters from Mir: An Astronaut's Letter to His Son.* New York: McGraw-Hill, 2003. American astronaut Jerry Linenger's letters home are an eloquent expression of his love for his young son. Written from space station *Mir,* they are also full of many fascinating details of life in space.

Robert Taylor, *Life Aboard the Space Shuttle.* San Diego, CA: Lucent Books, 2002. Another book in The Way People Live series, *Life Aboard the Space Shuttle* takes readers on an in-depth tour of one of the spaceships used to send astronauts to the International Space Station. The many astronaut quotes help to bring launch preparations, liftoff, space travel, and landing to life.

Web Sites

British National Space Centre (www.bnsc.gov.uk). A good source of information about the space shuttle.

Discovery Channel (dsc.discovery.com). The Web site of the Discovery Channel has many space-related features, including news stories about the International Space Station and the spacecraft that service it.

European Space Agency (www.esa.int). Contains general information about the International Space Station, describes life aboard the station, and provides news of missions involving the station's European partners.

Exploratorium: The Museum of Science, Art and Human Perception (www.exploratorium.com). The Web site of San Francisco's Exploratorium, a hands-on science museum, contains many articles and interactive features about space-based science, including scientific research conducted aboard the International Space Station.

The First African in Space Project (www.africaninspace.com). Maintained by the company of the second tourist in space, Mark Shuttleworth, this site features Shuttleworth's diary entries about his trip to the International Space Station and his training for the journey at Star City, Russia.

Florida Today Space News (www.floridatoday.com/news/space/index.htm). This online newspaper focuses on spaceflight news from NASA's Kennedy Space Center. It also maintains archives of previous news stories related to spaceflight.

How Stuff Works (www.howstuffworks.com). This Web site explains the inner workings of every subject imaginable, including space stations, space shuttles, space suits, and the process of becoming an astronaut.

Humans in Space, NASA (www.nasa.gov/vision/space/features/index.html). This comprehensive Web site—one of many separate sites maintained by NASA—offers a complete overview of humans in space, including news of current space station missions, and many features detailing what it is like to live and work in space.

Human Space Flight—International Space Station, NASA (spaceflight.nasa.gov/station). The International Space Station section of NASA's Human Space Flight Web site provides updated statistics on the station, progress reports, and news from station crews.

Human Space Flight—Space Station Gallery (www.spaceflight.nasa.gov/gallery/images/station/index.html). The title does not do justice to the resources available at this NASA Web site. The site is full of pictures as well as streaming videos made by the astronauts of every ISS mission. Included are demonstrations of many aspects of living and working in space, such as food preparation and space walking.

NASA Johnson Space Center (www.jsc.nasa.gov). Johnson Space Center is the home of NASA's human spaceflight activities. This site contains a wealth of information about the space shuttles, the International Space Station, astronauts, and much more.

Neurolab, NASA (neurolab.jsc.nasa.gov). One of many Web sites maintained by NASA, the Neurolab site reports on NASA research into the effects of space travel on the human nervous system.

Russian Aviation and Space Agency (www.rosaviakosmos.ru/english/eindex.htm). The English-language section of the Russian Space Agency Web site offers a brief overview of some of the agency's activities.

Science & Space, CNN.com (www.cnn.com/TECH/space). CNN's science and space Web site covers shuttle, Soyuz, space station, and other space-related stories.

Science@NASA (science.nasa.gov). Dedicated to space-based science, this NASA Web site includes information about the day-to-day experience of living aboard the International Space Station.

Space.com (www.space.com). This site provides up-to-the-minute news and keeps an extensive archive of all topics related to space, including the Russian, U.S., and Chinese space agencies and space stations.

Space News (www.spacenews.com). Continually updated, this site provides news and commentary on all aspects of spaceflight.

Space Ref—Space News as It Happens (www.spaceref.com). A portal to breaking space news, this Web site also provides original news coverage and commentary.

Space Station: A Rare Inside View of the Next Frontier in Space Exploration (www.pbs.org/spacestation). This PBS site is devoted to the International Space Station, including details of astronaut training.

Story Musgrave (www.spacestory.com). The Web site of astronaut Story Musgrave contains interviews, journals, and other material about his experiences in space.

Texas Aerospace Scholars, Johnson Space Center and the State of Texas (aerospacescholars.jsc.nasa.gov). NASA's Johnson Space Center and the State of Texas maintain this educational site for middle school, high school, and community college students.

UK National Measurement Laboratory (www.npl.co.uk). The Web site of the United Kingdom's National Measurement Laboratory defines concepts in the physical sciences, including g forces.

U.S. Air Force Academy (www.usafa.af.mil). The Web site of the U.S. Air Force Academy includes basic information on the effect of g forces on high-performance aircraft pilots.

Works Consulted

Books

Bryan Burrough, *Dragonfly: NASA and the Crisis Aboard the* Mir. New York: HarperCollins, 1998. Journalist Bryan Burrough details the growing pains of the first joint American-Russian space station program, the missions to Russian space station *Mir* in the late 1990s. Included are many captivating eyewitness accounts of life aboard the station and a section of full-color photographs.

David M. Harland and John E. Catchpole, *Creating the International Space Station.* New York: Springer, 2002. This book details not only the building and operation of the most ambitious space station yet, but also covers all the stations that came before it and details how they paved the way for the ISS.

Kerry Mark Joëls, Gregory P. Kennedy, and David Larkin, *The Space Shuttle Operator's Manual.* New York: Ballantine, 1982. Lavishly illustrated and designed to resemble an automobile owner's manual, this book is an easy-to-read reference work describing procedures for launching and landing the space shuttle, operating the onboard systems while in orbit, and many other topics, including how to put on and use a space suit.

Kevin W. Kelley, ed., *The Home Planet.* Reading, MA: Addison-Wesley, 1988. Kelley presents 150 oversized pages of breathtaking photographs of Earth taken from space, along with running commentary from astronauts of many different nationalities.

Valentin Lebedev, *Diary of a Cosmonaut: 211 Days in Space.* Trans. Luba Diangar. Eds. Daniel Puckett and C.N. Harrison. New York: Bantam Books, 1988. A detailed and very personal account of life aboard *Salyut-7,* the last of the Salyut series of Russian space stations.

Richard S. Lewis, *Appointment on the Moon: The Full Story of Americans in Space from* Explorer 1 *to the Lunar Landing and Beyond,* rev. ed. New York: Ballantine, 1969. A good overview of the early history of the U.S. space program, this book features a detailed treatment of the concepts involved in space travel, including how rockets work and how spacecraft and stations stay in orbit.

Jerry M. Linenger, *Off the Planet: Surviving Five Perilous Months Aboard the Space Station* Mir. New York: McGraw-Hill, 2000. American astronaut Jerry Linenger presents a harrowing firsthand account of life aboard the aging space station *Mir.* The book is illustrated with two sections of color photographs.

Robert Zimmerman, *Leaving Earth: Space Stations, Rival Superpowers, and the Quest for Interplanetary Travel.* Washington, DC: Joseph Henry Press, 2003. A complete history of space stations, from early concepts through the International Space Station. Based on hundreds of interviews with astronauts, scientists, and other participants in the building and operation of space stations, this is a very thorough account.

Periodicals

Sharon LaFraniere and Kathy Sawyer, "Astronauts Describe Harrowing Descent," *Washington Post,* May 6, 2003.

James Oberg, "China's Great Leap Upward," *Scientific American,* October 2003.

Jim Yardley, "After 21 Hours, Chinese Spacecraft Lands Safely," *New York Times*, October 16, 2003.

Film and Television

Mission to Mir, directed by Ivan Gallin. 1997. Burbank, CA: Warner Home video, 2001. Spectacular footage of the first joint U.S./Russian missions to the space station *Mir*, showing astronaut training, rocket launches, arriving at the station, life aboard the station, and returning to Earth. The film is narrated by several station astronauts, including Shannon Lucid, the record holder for time spent in space by a woman.

Out of the Present. Paris: K-Films, 1996. An artful presentation of life aboard Russian space station *Mir* during the collapse of the Soviet Union. Included are Soyuz docking footage and scenes of life aboard the station.

Terror in Space, NOVA. Boston: WGBH-TV, 1998. Produced and aired only a year after the fact, this PBS program combines interviews, video footage, and computer graphics to tell the stories of the fire and collision on space station *Mir*.

Internet Sources

John E. Blaha, "John E. Blaha," NASA Oral History, ISS Phase I History Project, 1998. http://spaceflight.nasa.gov/history/shuttle-mir/people/p-r-blaha.htm.

Kenneth Chang, "Riding the Vomit Comet," ABCNews.com, March 26, 1999. http://abcnews.go.com/sections/science/DailyNews/vomitcomet 990326_flight.html.

Keith Cowing, "Earth's First Self-Financed Astronaut," SpaceRef.com, December 10, 2000. www.spaceref.com/news/viewnews.html?id=263.

"Fire Prevention in Space," NASA Human Exploration and Development of Space Enterprise, 2001. http://spaceresearch.nasa.gov/sts-107/resourceguide/content/science/bioreactor/info/k-12info.pdf.

Ed Lu, "The Soyuz Ride," NASA Human Space Flight Web site, http://spaceflight.nasa.gov/station/crew/exp7/luletters/lu_letter1.html.

Shannon W. Lucid, "Shannon W. Lucid," NASA Oral History, ISS Phase I History Project, 1998. http://spaceflight.nasa.gov/history/shuttle-mir/people/p-r-lucid.htm.

Jim Oberg, "News in Space," ABCNews.com. http://abcnews.go.com/sections/science/DailyNews.

Norman E. Thagard, "Norman E. Thagard," NASA Oral History, ISS Phase I History Project, 1998. http://spaceflight.nasa.gov/history/shuttle-mir/people/p-r-thagard.htm.

Index

ABC News, 14
accidents, 21, 72
  see also emergencies
adaptation, to space travel, 22–23
  see also requirements, for astronauts; weightlessness
advertising, 62
Aleksandrov, Aleksandr, 23
Allen, Joseph, 21, 23
astronauts, 12–14
  see also names of astronauts; space station; *and specific activities and situations*
Atlantis (space shuttle), 24, 93
attitude control systems, 69

Baikonur Cosmodrome, 19
Beregovoy, Georgi, 22–23
biology experiments, 52
Blaha, John, 30–31, 79–80
boosting, 45
Bowersox, Kenneth
  Columbia (space shuttle) disaster and, 72
  on effects of life in space, 95
  on readjustment to gravity, 91, 92
  on recreation aboard space station, 75
  on reentry to Earth's atmosphere, 88
  on spacewalking view, 59–60
  on telephoning home from space station, 77
  on touchdown of space shuttle, 90
  on weekends aboard space station, 75
Budarin, Nikolai, 72, 90

cargo shuttles, 46–47
Carr, Gerry
  on activation of *Skylab* (space station), 31
  on adapting to weightlessness, 39
  on communicating with home, 77
  on docking process, 27–28
  on entertainment in space, 47
  on impact of life in space, 35
  on jetpack, 62
  on readjustment to gravity, 92
  on shaving in space, 42
  on spacewalking, 61

celebrations, 77–78
centrifuge, 16
Challenger (space shuttle), 21
Chang, Kenneth, 14–15
Chinese spacecraft, 18
cleaning, 44–46
Columbia (space shuttle), 21, 72
connecting. *See* docking
construction work, 56–57
cooking, 37–38
cosmonauts, 12–14
  see also names of cosmonauts; space station; *and specific activities and situations*
crewmates, 42
crew return vehicle, 74
crises. *See* accidents; emergencies

departure. *See* launch
Diary of a Cosmonaut: 211 Days in Space (Lebedev), 48, 84
disasters, 21, 72
  see also emergencies
docking, 25, 27–30

Earth legs, 90
Edwards Air Force Base, 88
Elektron, 45
e-mail, 77
embarkation. *See* launch
emergencies
  decompression, 67–68
  escape from the space station, 72–74
  fires, 64–67
  medical problems, 70–72
  power failures, 68–70
  space shuttle disasters, 72
exercise, 53, 80–81, 83
experiments, 51–53
extravehicular activity (EVA), 57–61

floating. *See* weightlessness
Foale, Michael
  on collision on *Mir*, 67
  on life aboard *Mir*, 33–34
  on odor of space station, 31
  power restoration aboard *Mir* and, 70
  on space station toilet, 41
  on ventilation failure aboard *Mir*, 70
food, 37–38, 40–41
foot restraints, 61

g (gravity) forces, 15–16, 88
Gagarin, Yuri, 19
garbage, 42–44
Gibson, Ed, 42
glovebox, 56

ham radio, 77
handholds, 60–61
heat shields, 89
Hermaszewski, Miroslav, 21
holidays, 77–78
housekeeping, 44–46
hygiene, 42–46, 49

interconnectedness, 95
International Space Station (ISS), 10, 24, 34
  see also space station

jetpacks, 62
jobs, 51–63
Johnson Space Center, 12–13

Kennedy Space Center, 19
Kerwin, Joe, 31–32
Korzun, Valeri, 66–67

launch, 18–21
laundry, 42–43
Lazutkin, Sasha, 65–66, 67
leaks, 67–68
Lebedev, Valentin
  on light shows in space, 48
  on plant growing in space, 52
  on radiation effect in space, 84
  on readjustment to gravity, 92
  on shuttle supply craft, 46
  on sleeping in space, 50
  on spacewalking, 59
lifelines, 61
Linenger, Jerry M.
  on cargo ship departure, 44
  on classroom training, 12–13
  on departing from *Mir,* 87
  on docking with space station, 30–31
  on effect of life in space, 95
  on exercise aboard space station, 80–81
  on fire aboard *Mir,* 66
  on *Mir*, 24, 34
  on moving while weightless, 37

on prospect of returning to Earth, 85
on resonance aboard *Mir*, 83
on sleeping and carbon dioxide, 50
on smoke inhalation emergency aboard *Mir*, 70
on space shuttle launch, 20
spacewalking and, 60
on Star City training, 13–14
on teeth brushing in space, 49
on vacuuming in space, 45
on writing letters from space, 48–49
Lu, Ed, 19
Lucid, Shannon W.
on food in space, 37–38
on life in space, 35, 36
as narrator of film, 37–38
on opening new space station module, 57
on reading books in space, 78–79
on returning home, 92, 94

materials science experiments, 51, 55–56
meals, 37–38, 40–41
medical experiments, 51–53, 82
microbes, 45–46
Microgravity Science Glovebox, 56
microorganisms, 45–46
Mir (space station)
achievements of, 33
docking with, 30–31
early missions of, 10
fire aboard, 54–67
launch of, 20
political situation and landing zone for, 69
power failure and, 69–70
training for, 13–14
see also space station
mishaps. *See* accidents; emergencies
mock-ups, 17–18
music, 76

National Aeronautics and Space Administration (NASA), 18
Neutral Buoyancy Laboratory (NBL), 14
news conferences, 61–62
Newton, Isaac, 16

observation, 53–55
oxygen, 45

paying passengers, 62–63
Pettit, Donald, 72, 90
Phantom Torso, 82
physical requirements, 12
plant growing, 52
plasma, 88
practice. *See* training
pressure suits. *See* space suits
Progress (cargo shuttle), 46
psychological requirements, 12
public relations, 61–62

radiation, 82, 83–84
readjustment to gravity, 90–92
recreation, 47–49, 78–80
reentry, into Earth's atmosphere, 87–88, 89
requirements, for astronauts, 12
research, 51–56
resistive exercise device (RED), 83
resonance, 81, 83
resting, 49–50
resupply, 46–47
Russian Space Agency (RSA), 18

Salyut-1 (space station), 10, 26
scientific research, 52–56
Shenzhou (spacecraft), 18
shower, 42
Shuttleworth, Mark, 62–63
sightseers, 62–63
Simplified Aid for EVA Rescue (SAFER), 61
Skylab (space station), 29
sleeping, 49–50
smoke detectors, 66
Sonny Carter Training Facility, 14
Soyuz (spacecraft), 18, 21–22, 72–74, 93
spacecraft, 18
  see also space shuttle; space station
space shuttle
  astronaut tasks aboard, 24
  disasters of, 21
  disengagement of, from space station, 34
  docking of, with space station, 25, 27–31
  function of, 24
  landing runways for, 93
  purpose of, 18
space station, 32–34
  activation of, 31
  astronaut adjustments to, 31
  balance of activities aboard, 75
  communication with home from, 75, 77

departing from, 86–87
eating aboard, 37–38, 40–41
emergencies aboard, 64–74
escaping from, 72–74
exercise aboard, 53, 80
experiments aboard, 51–53
garbage handling aboard, 42–44
holidays aboard, 77–78
hygiene aboard, 42–46
music and, 76
orbit maintenance and, 45
oxygen aboard, 45
packing for departure from, 85–86
paying passengers aboard, 62–63
radiation hazard aboard, 84
return to Earth from, 85–95
sleeping aboard, 49–50
toilet aboard, 41
work aboard, 75
space suits, 14, 19
Space Vehicle mock-ups, 17–18
spacewalking, 24, 47–61, 58
spacewalking suit, 58
Star City (Russia), 12, 13–14
supply shuttles, 46–47

takeoff. *See* launch
telephoning, 75, 77
telescopes, 53–55
Thagard, Norman, 10, 71–72
Tito, Dennis, 62–63
toilet, 41
touchdown, of space shuttle, 88, 90
tourists, 62–63
tragedies, 21, 72
training
classroom, 12–14
gravity forces and, 15–16
mock-ups and, 17–18
simulators and, 16–17
weightlessness and, 14–15
trash, 42–44
Tsibliyev, Vasily, 70

vestibular system, 91
videos, 61–62
Vomit Comet, 14

water, 24, 41, 42, 45
weightlessness, 21

adapting to, 22–23, 37, 39
buoyancy and, 14
eating and, 41
exercise and, 80–81, 83
orbit and, 16
training for, 14–15
wing walking, 60–61
work, 51–63

zero gravity. *See* weightlessness

Picture Credits

Cover: National Aeronautics and Space Administration (NASA)
Sergei Karpukhin/EPA/Landov, 90
NASA, 11, 13, 15, 17, 20, 22, 25, 28, 30, 33, 36, 39, 40, 41, 43, 44, 47, 48, 49, 52, 53, 54, 55, 59, 60, 65, 68, 71, 73, 76, 78, 79, 81, 82, 86, 87, 89, 93, 94
© Roger Ressmeyer/CORBIS, 26
Time Life Pictures/Getty Images, 29
Shamil Zhumatov/Reuters/Landov, 91

About the Author

Michael Belfiore has written about spaceflight for numerous periodicals and reference works including *Chronogram, Encyclopedia of World Biography,* and the *New York Post.* He lives and works with his wife, fellow writer Wendy Kagan, in Woodstock, New York. Look for him on the Web at http://www.michaelbelfiore.com.